GRENVILLE GOODWIN AMONG THE WESTERN APACHE

May 14, 1933

17 Broadmoor Ave.
Colo. Spgs.
Colo.

Dear Morris,

Am writing to send you that book reference I told you about. It is —— Official Correspondence of James S. Calhoun, While Indian Agent at Santa Fe 185: - 1857, Pub. by U.S. Dept. of Interior, Washington, D.C. This may not be the absolutely correct title but you can find it by this anyway.

It was nice to see you again at Las Cruces, and have a chance to talk. Sometime when things are a little further advanced, I want to get together with you and spend about a week just going over our material from A to Z and making comparisons so that what one of us has missed, the other may be able to give a lead on, etc.

GRENVILLE GOODWIN
Among the Western Apache

Letters From the Field

Morris E. Opler, *Editor*

THE UNIVERSITY OF ARIZONA PRESS
Tucson, Arizona

About Grenville Goodwin . . .

GRENVILLE GOODWIN, born in New York state in 1907, developed an affection for the Southwest and its native peoples during a college preparatory course in Arizona. Health problems prevented further formal schooling, yet Goodwin achieved an enviable reputation in American ethnology. He obtained a position at a trading post and began to build a note file that has become a rich source of information about the Western Apache. By the time of his sudden death in 1940, he had published six journal articles and a book of Western Apache myths and tales. *Social Organization of the Western Apache,* a major work dealing with this theme, was published posthumously and reissued (UA Press, 1969) after long being out of print. Since its original 1942 publication, scholars have edited and published some of Goodwin's notes and papers. The bulk of the remaining material has been deposited at the University of Arizona where editing was begun by Keith Basso, with the book *Western Apache Raiding and Warfare* as the first fruit of that venture (UA Press, 1971). Anthropologists' appreciation of the scope of Goodwin's achievement continues to grow.

About the Editor . . .

MORRIS OPLER has devoted much of his long professional career to research dealing with the seven Apachean-speaking tribes of the American Southwest and the southern Plains. His interest in Apache field research resulted in a close professional friendship, principally carried on by written correspondence, with researcher Grenville Goodwin. Holder of a doctorate in anthropology from the University of Chicago, Opler is known for his contributions to anthropological theory as well as for his ethnographic work. His published works include numerous books, monographs, and journal articles. He has received many awards and honors and has served as president of the American Anthropological Association. Professor Emeritus of Cornell University, he has continued to teach and to pursue research as Professor of Anthropology at the University of Oklahoma.

THE UNIVERSITY OF ARIZONA PRESS

I. S. B. N.-0-8165-0417-2
L. C. No. 73-85723

Contents

Foreword, *by Keith H. Basso* 7

Introduction 11

Key to Symbols 18

The Letters
  (City unknown)
     February 23, 1932 19

  Santa Fe, New Mexico
     February 29, 1932 21

  Bylas, Arizona
     March 22, 1932 22
     April 4, 1932 24
     April 15, 1932 30

  Colorado Springs, Colorado
     May 14, 1933 33
     May 22, 1933 34
     October 15, 1933 35
     January 8, 1934 47
     January (n.d.) 1934 50
     February 2, 1934 58
     February 19, 1934 63

  Santa Fe, New Mexico
     September 5, 1934 65

Bylas, Arizona
    June 2, 1935 68
    July 11, 1935 70

Colorado Springs, Colorado
    July 28, 1935 74
    August 12, 1936 76

Tucson, Arizona
    February 6, 1937 78
    February 10, 1937 81
    March 13, 1937 83
    May 3, 1937 85

Santa Fe, New Mexico
    July 25, 1938 87
    October 22, 1938 91

Tucson, Arizona
    November 13, 1938 93

Chicago, Illinois
    October 1, 1939 95

Bibliographic References 97

Acknowledgments 99

Index 101

ILLUSTRATIONS

Fig. 1. Horned cap 32
Fig. 2. Main Western Apache house types 60
Fig. 3. Differences in house frames 61
Fig. 4. a. Plains type man's shirt; b. Woman's skirt as
depicted on Lipan doll; c. Woman's high moccasin
as depicted on Lipan doll; d. Woman's hair style as
depicted on Lipan doll; e. Cradleboard erroneously
alleged to be Lipan 89

Foreword

IN THE LATE 1920s Grenville Goodwin, the anthropologist whose letters form the contents of this volume, embarked upon a long-range program of linguistic and ethnographic research among the Western Apache Indians of Arizona. Although Goodwin was not the first social scientist to become interested in these people, he was unquestionably the most dedicated and thorough, and by the time of his death in 1940 he was intimately familiar with virtually every aspect of Western Apache culture.

Goodwin died prematurely at the age of thirty-three, having published only a few brief articles and a collection of Western Apache myths. Fortunately, he had also finished the manuscript for a book that would later be recognized as his finest work and a major contribution to American Indian ethnology. This was *The Social Organization of the Western Apache,* a lengthy and richly detailed study, published posthumously in 1942 and brought back into print in 1969, which represented the first successful attempt to describe Western Apache society as an orderly, integrated system.

The remainder of Goodwin's ethnographic materials, including voluminous notes on Apache subsistence practices, material culture, and religion, remained in the hands of his widow, Mrs. Janice Massey, until 1969 when she graciously presented them to the Arizona State Museum, University of Arizona, with the understanding that they would be prepared for publication. One volume, entitled *Western Apache Raiding and Warfare,* appeared in 1971 and several others are planned. Our knowledge of Western Apache culture is still incomplete, but thanks to Goodwin's meticulous records it continues to grow.

At approximately the same time that Grenville Goodwin took up residence with the Western Apache, another young anthropologist, Morris E. Opler, began field research among the Chiricahua and Mescalero Apache in New Mexico. Opler, like Goodwin, was keenly aware that earlier studies were deficient. He also saw that the opportunity to be instructed in Apache culture by individuals who had participated fully in pre-reservation life would soon be lost. Moved by a sense of urgency and endowed with an immense capacity for hard work, Opler plunged deeply into his research. After completing studies of the Chiricahua and Mescalero, he went on to investigate the Jicarilla and Lipan Apache. By 1940 he had firmly established himself as an excellent ethnographer, an innovative anthropological theorist, and the world's foremost authority on Apachean cultures. By the 1970s the situation had not changed. Morris Opler continued to pursue his long-standing interests with undiminished vigor. The quality of his work remains exceptionally high, and he continues to make important theoretical contributions. In the 1970s, more than ever before, he is the dean of Apachean ethnology.

Grenville Goodwin and Morris Opler met for the first time in 1931. The two men took an immediate liking to each other and soon struck up a correspondence for the purpose of exchanging ideas and information about their research. More was involved than mutual respect and curiosity, for, as Opler points out in his Introduction to this volume, both he and Goodwin were convinced that a systematic comparison of Apachean cultures was long overdue and that such a comparison would yield significant results. Thus, although Goodwin and Opler were working separately, they also were working together. Sustained by a common sense of exploration and discovery, and concerned with a similar set of empirical problems, they were joined in the belief that they were contributing to a more powerful and scientific discipline of anthropology. In this respect history was to prove them correct, and therefore Goodwin's letters to Opler are doubly valuable. On the one hand, the letters make public factual data on a wide variety of Western Apache beliefs and customs. On the other, they reveal Goodwin's increasingly sophisticated thoughts — many of them directly influenced by Opler — about how to analyze these materials. In short, Goodwin's correspondence represents a contribution to the development of American anthropology as well as to Apachean studies.

The reader should keep in mind that Goodwin's letters were not intended for the layman. They were meant for a fellow specialist who held firmly to the assumption that sound cultural description necessarily rests upon a solid foundation of ethnographic detail. Consequently, emphasis is placed upon the particular rather than the general, upon the careful reporting of empirical facts rather than mercurial flights of theoretical speculation. Western Apache kin terms and place names, the relationship of agriculture to the evolution of clans, ceremonial symbolism, marriage practices, and the manufacture of items of material culture are some of the topics with which Goodwin deals. If his letters do not present an overall picture of Western Apache culture, they more than make up for it by providing precious information that was heretofore unavailable. Enhanced by Opler's introductory remarks and footnotes, *Grenville Goodwin Among the Western Apache: Letters From the Field* constitutes an important addition to the ethnography of an intricate — and in some ways unique — American Indian society. Serious students of the contemporary Western Apache, together with those concerned with understanding the history of this group, owe to Goodwin and Opler a debt of lasting gratitude.

KEITH H. BASSO

Introduction

GRENVILLE GOODWIN was one of the most gifted and effective field anthropologists in the history of the discipline. The letters of this present collection constitute a record of his professional development. They cover the seven years of his short life during which he engaged in intensive work among the people in whom he was so interested and for whom he had so much regard. They include important ethnological detail, given in response to a co-worker's questions, some of which never reached his notebooks. What is more important, they put many topics, on which he did not live to express himself in books and papers, in context as he saw them. They yield facts on the history of Southwestern ethnology which should be preserved. They give life and body to his raw notes, which are now being so admirably edited by Keith Basso and his assistants (Goodwin 1971).

In the summer of 1929 I received a small travel grant from the University of Buffalo, where I was then studying, which enabled me to investigate research possibilities in the American Southwest. I had just completed my undergraduate studies and had resolved to become an anthropologist. It was during this exploratory trip that I made my first contact with the Apache and decided to make them the focus of my graduate research. In the year that followed, I brought together the scattered and often contradictory materials about these peoples in a Master's thesis. The venture only confirmed my feeling that contemporary field work among the Apache was desperately needed. In the late summer of 1930 I left for the University of Chicago to continue graduate study. The opportunity to return to the Apache came sooner than I anticipated. A summer

11

field training party, sponsored by the Laboratory of Anthropology of Santa Fe, was to carry on research under the direction of Professor Ruth Benedict at the Mescalero Apache Indian Reservation in New Mexico, and I was awarded a fellowship which enabled me to participate in the program. The other fellowship holders were John P. Gillin, Jules Henry, Regina Flannery Herzfeld, and Sol Tax — an extraordinarily able and congenial group, all of whom later became prominent in the profession. Harry Hoijer, who was by this time instructing in linguistics at the University of Chicago, joined the party to help train the members in linguistic techniques. For the rest of the students this was essentially a training course in field methods; because of my commitment and previous immersion in Apache study, it was something additional to me. At the conclusion of the summer's work it was decided that I should receive copies of my companions' field notes to enrich my own store, and a grant from the Southwest Society enabled me to remain in the field for some time after the others had scattered to their homes. I arrived in Chicago late for the fall quarter but tremendously excited by the discoveries made and the possibilities uncovered. I thought of myself as a pioneer in modern Apachean studies.

What I did not know was that in 1929, too, a young man of just my own age had become equally interested in the Apache and by the fall of 1931 had gathered a considerable amount of information about the Western Apache of Arizona. This other enthusiast was Grenville Goodwin. In the late fall or early winter of 1931, at a time when I was busy reviewing my field notes and outlining what was to become my doctoral dissertation, Goodwin stopped at Chicago on his way east, and we met for the first time. He had heard that someone who had been at Mescalero was now in residence at Chicago, and he wanted to compare experiences with a kindred spirit. Actually, he first made contact with Sol Tax, who, in view of my continuing Apache interests, urged him to talk to me.

Because of a health problem, Goodwin's formal education had been interrupted, and he lacked the technical vocabulary and sense of problem of the trained student in anthropology. At this point it was the material culture of the Western Apache about which he had most organized knowledge. He showed me a notebook of meticulously drawn sketches in color of Apache artifacts which he had found in various museums. Later he sent me photostats from this collection which pertained to the tribes in which I had become particularly interested. In addition to his rather precise knowledge of Western Apache material culture, Goodwin possessed a good deal of sound but diffused information about other aspects of their life. What he lacked was some kind of ground plan, especially in respect to nonmaterial culture, which would help him to systematize and extend his research. Yet it was obvious that he was intelligent, dedicated, completely honest and sincere, eager to learn, and temperamentally equipped for his task. He already controlled an Apachean language to a surprising degree, and since his doctors advised him to camp out in Arizona as much as possible, he had unusual field opportunities.

A large part of my own early Apache material had to do with social organization. My thesis director was A. R. Radcliffe-Brown, who was urging the comparative study of social organization upon American ethnologists, and in the division of labor during the Laboratory of Anthropology field party I had been permitted to concentrate upon this general topic. Goodwin asked if he could read my materials, which, through my wife's secretarial skills, had been neatly typed and filed in labeled folders. He spent several days, perhaps the better part of a week, carefully reading the data and making copious notes. At intervals he peppered me with questions about the gathering and interpretation of the materials. A fresh line of inquiry had been opened to him. He put down any number of research leads in his "question book" and vowed that he would gather comparable data from the Western Apache on his return to the field. I heartily encouraged him in this resolve, for by this time I was well aware of the enormous task that carrying on research among the other Apache tribes would be, and I was delighted with the prospect of having so congenial and able a field worker doing parallel research farther west. Before we parted company, we agreed to write to each other and share information, to answer each other's inquiries, to keep our files open to each other for comparative purposes, and to meet and exchange views whenever possible. There are references in the letters to several of the meetings we managed to arrange. Mainly, however, we kept in touch by correspondence, and the letters I received, so rich in data, went into my Apache file.

When the outbreak of World War II disrupted my teaching career and forced a number of moves, I found that I had to reduce my possessions and put most of them in storage. In the case of Goodwin's letters (Goodwin had died several years before), only those portions which were ethnological in content were retained. Since most of our correspondence had centered around our field work, a large percentage of the letters have been preserved in entirety. In four cases, a part of a letter is missing, presumably devoted to personal matters. A portion of the goods which I put in storage mysteriously disappeared and was never recovered. I cannot be sure that some of the Goodwin letters were not in the missing packages, but the account given by those that are available seems to be reasonably consecutive. Twenty-five letters or parts of letters are left. Thirteen are handwritten, and the rest are typed. I have called the collection "Letters From the Field" because they emphasize the discoveries and problems of the ongoing field work, although only five were actually written from a field station. Most of the remainder were written (often in response to a message from me which he found waiting) just after Goodwin emerged from the field or during an enforced rest between field trips.

Goodwin's relations with people, Indians or whites, were relaxed, and in these informal letters he wrote as he spoke. To preserve his easy manner, I have edited the material as sparingly as possible. References that might otherwise be obscure are explained in footnotes. Since the letters were often written in haste to accommodate an impatient friend, no great pains were taken with spelling and punctuation; mechanical slips such as these have been corrected. Yet in regard to matters of substance, Goodwin was careful and thorough in these letters, as in all his work. He knew the natural setting to which the Apache had adjusted in all its moods. He was well read in the comparative ethnology of the Southwest, as his letters will attest. He entered the field at a time when there were old Apache present who had lived under aboriginal conditions, and he succeeded in gaining their confidence as few others could. He had a sense of mission and a quiet confidence in his ability ultimately to furnish a full account of all aspects of Western Apache culture. It was ironic that after overcoming one serious illness, and with his goal within his grasp, he should succumb at the age of thirty-three to another, unexpected scourge. Had he been spared to live a normal span of life, his contribution would have been epic. Even so, it is extremely substantial, and with the editing and publication of his field notes, his reputation continues to grow.

With two exceptions, I have no copies of the letters I wrote to Goodwin; the others probably were handwritten. One that I have is my long comment on the first draft of his manuscript dealing with Western Apache social organization; apparently I thought this was important enough to warrant having it typed and preserving a carbon. The second is a reply to his letters of July 25 and October 22, 1938. I have not sought to learn whether any of the others are still in existence; in any case, they would not be important in the present context. I have lived to write at length about the Apache tribes I have studied, an opportunity and satisfaction which were denied the gentle friend whose achievements and thoughts are given voice in the pages that follow.

MORRIS E. OPLER

The Letters

Key to Symbols Used by Goodwin
in Recording Apache Words

A RAISED PERIOD (·) following a vowel indicates that it is long. Nasalization of a vowel is shown by a subscript hook (ą). Western Apache dialects employ pitch accent or tone. The pitch of a syllable is carried by its vowel or by a syllabic "n." An acute accent (′) denotes high tone; a grave accent (ˋ), low tone. Glottal stops or sharp glottal closures can occur initially, medially, or terminally in a word. Raised clockwise hooks (ʼ) mark their presence. Certain consonants can be glottalized or pronounced with a simultaneous glottal closure. The raised clockwise hook directly over the consonant or between the letters of a consonantal cluster serves to symbolize these glottalized consonants. Besides the ordinary "l" there is a voiceless spirantal alveolar lateral or "barred l" (ł), which is similar in sound to the Welsh "ll." A voiced palatal spirant, often confused by an English-speaking listener with "y," is rendered by the gamma (γ). A raised counterclockwise hook (ʻ) is employed to designate aspiration or breath release.

M. E. O.

February 23, 1932[1]

... I'm sure the Field Museum would be willing to take a photostat of the buckskin and send it to him if he would write them and say just what he wanted it for, don't you think so? I don't have its catalogue number, or I would send it to him. It might seem to Blumensohn that I was holding out on him, which, of course, I would not want him to think, but I guess you can see my point about the matter.[2]

Well, to go on, I certainly hope that you will find something out about the type of *gá·n* headdress shown in the picture. They are distinctly of a coloring and type which I have never seen on the San Carlos and Ft. Apache reservations, though, of course, they may come from these reservations and be something which I have not yet run across. Also, as I told you, the Coyotero claim that the Chiricahua Apache and Victorio's people used to use ornate headdresses of this type, which, of course, may or may not be true.[3] At any rate, this would be an interesting thing to follow out, don't you think?

As soon as I get the Chiricahua relationship terms from those Chiricahua residing on the San Carlos Res., I will send them to you.[4]

---

[1] The beginning and end of this letter are missing. Its date, but not the place from which it was written, was noted on the part retained. Following our initial meeting in Chicago, Goodwin apparently was back in the West again and ready to resume field work. Letters that were disposed of probably preceded this one. See footnote 2.

[2] Jules Blumensohn, who later changed his surname to Henry, had been a member of the Laboratory of Anthropology summer field party of 1931 and had been particularly interested in Apache ceremonialism and religious symbolism. Goodwin had shown me a drawing of a painted Apache ritual buckskin which I thought would interest Blumensohn. It was a question of how best to get a picture of this object to him. The wording suggests that Goodwin and I had been in correspondence before the arrival of this first surviving letter.

[3] Goodwin had supplied me with a picture of his sketches of two masked dancer headdresses which were catalogued as Chiricahua Apache at the Heye Museum in New York. They were much more ornate (a Western Apache characteristic) than an Chiricahua examples with which I was familiar, and Chiricahua informants to whom I showed the picture consistently rejected them as Chiricahua handiwork.

[4] I was interested in learning whether older Chiricahua who had intermarried with the Western Apache had adopted Western Apache kinship usages, especially those related to clan organization, which was strong among the Western Apache and lacking among the Chiricahua.

I leave here for San Carlos this next Wednesday or Thursday and am planning to put in the next several months working with the Coyotero — maybe, if all goes well, till next fall sometime. It is my desire to make this work on the Coyotero as complete as possible, in every way. If it is possible to bring out a publication on the Coyotero successfully, then of course what I want to do is to work on the other divisions of the Western Apache — Tonto, Arivaipa, and Cibecue — but all this is a long way in the future, as you may well understand.[5]

If you and I can pull together on . . .[6]

---

[5] The units which Goodwin here calls "divisions" were themselves composed of bands but had not yet differentiated into separate tribes. In later work he calls them "groups," and Basso (1970: 2, 5) now refers to them as "subtribal groups." Goodwin ultimately substituted the name "White Mountain Apache" for "Coyotero Apache." The term "Arivaipa" was dropped in favor of "San Carlos," and the Tonto were divided into Northern Tonto and Southern Tonto. For his final conception of the Western Apache subtribal units, see Goodwin 1942: 4–5.

[6] Unfortunately I disposed of the page on which Goodwin indicated what he hoped would be accomplished by our cooperation. He obviously began in an optimistic vein, however.

Feb. 29, 1932
Santa Fe, New Mexico

Dear Opler,

Your letter came just the other day, and I guess by this time you have mine. It was mighty nice to hear from you, and thanks a lot for writing to Mrs. Parsons.[7]

Am pretty much interested to hear what your conclusions will be about locations of bands, etc., and also your relationship systems of both Mescalero and Chiricahua will be darned interesting to me. It will help out a lot if you put the man and woman speaking separately. I will make it the same way for you.

Have never heard of the Cibecue being called Pinal as yet. I should like very much to be able to read those Indian Affairs Repts., as should think they must have some good data in them. If that word "Pinal" should be applied to a certain group of Apache, due to their location, which it may or may not be, there is only this I can say: that there are only two localities which have ever gone, or still do go, by that name "Pinal." The first of these are the Pinal Mts. directly south and west of Globe, Ariz., in what was apparently the old country of the Arivaipa band. The second is the present Graham Mt., just south of the Gila River, near Safford, Ariz., which was formerly called Pinaleño Mt. and which lies in the old Eastern Coyotero range.[8] It was interesting that you should . . .[9]

---

[7] Elsie Clews Parsons, who was a philanthropist as well as an accomplished scholar, had, through her Southwest Society, provided some financial backing for my field work. I believe I called her attention to Goodwin's work in the hope that he might receive similar help. The Southwest Society, the organization through which Dr. Parsons encouraged research in the Southwest, later did contribute to the publication of Goodwin's *Myths and Tales of the White Mountain Apache* (1939).

[8] Earlier writers applied terms to Apache social units so loosely and inconsistently that it is often a major task to determine which branch of a tribe is being described. In later work Goodwin restricted his use of the term "Pinal" to a specific band of the San Carlos group.

[9] The latter part of this letter, too, is missing.

Mar. 22, 1932
Bylas, Arizona

Dear Opler,

Your letter with the money order and the one with the relationship terms came all right. Thanks for both.[10]

You may be sure that my files are open to you also, except only on such material which at present I have been asked to keep to myself by the men who told it to me.[11]

It's a long way ahead till next Sept., when you say you will be back at Mescalero, but I am keeping it in mind, so that we can get together for a talk then.[12]

About the locations of the Western Apache: it was easiest just to trace out the boundaries on a good road map. I have done this and sent it to you under separate cover, with full information as to the meaning of the markings on the map. I think it is what you wanted, and if not, let me know.[13]

About the girl's adolescence ceremony: the Coyotero always hold that part of the ceremony of which you speak in a tipi made only of four posts. I have seen the Cibecue hold it without any tipi at all, in the open.

The Tonto and Arivaipa girl's adolescence ceremony formerly may have differed a little from Cibecue and Coyotero ways, but at the present time the Tonto and Arivaipa go to the adolescence ceremonies conducted by Coyotero medicine men. I have never seen a ceremony for Tonto or Arivaipa girls conducted by a Tonto or Arivaipa medicine man so far, although I hope to before long.

---

[10] As I remember it, the money order was a repayment for the reproduction of drawings which Goodwin had obtained for me. By this time my Mescalero and Chiricahua kinship material had been checked, and I sent the terms on to Goodwin for his own information and for what help they would afford in his comparative research.

[11] Since I had opened my files to Goodwin in Chicago, I asked whether a similar courtesy would be extended to me if opportunity should arise. I may say that Goodwin always acted promptly and generously to any request I made for information.

[12] I planned to complete my formal work for the Ph.D. in the summer quarter of 1932 and to be in the field again in the fall of 1932. I was able to hold to this schedule although, because the degree could not be granted *in absentia* in those days, it was 1933 before I presented myself in person to obtain it.

[13] This map was very useful in roughing out the boundaries between the Western Apache and the Chiricahua and is still in existence.

The Navajo hold an adolescence ceremony for girls very similar to that of the Western Apache in some respects, from what I hear. I have never seen one personally but have heard about it from absolutely reliable persons on that subject. Just what kind of a structure is built for that part of the ceremony of which you speak, I cannot say for sure, but believe that it is the regular Navajo lodge, though which of the three oldest types of lodge I don't know. It may be any one of the three old types.[14]

You will be interested to know that I have answers for two of the questions which you put to me in Chicago. 1. The son-in-law obligation to father-in-law is the same over here among the Coyotero as that described to me by you as existing among the Chiricahua and Mescalero. 2. A boy is only obliged to observe certain taboos on his first war party; and on his second war party, or any thereafter, he is free from taboos. These taboos you already know.[15]

I have resumed my Apache work for the University of Arizona as before[16] and have been here working at Bylas for nearly three weeks now, working hard, and hope to be here for several months more — that is, on different parts of the reservations. Plants are beginning to bloom here now, and almost every . . .

---

[14] Differences I had discovered between the Mescalero and Chiricahua ceremonial structures for the girl's puberty rite prompted my question.

[15] During our Chicago sessions I put many comparative questions to Goodwin which he could not answer at the time but which he said he would pursue in the field. One of the gratifying aspects of our relationship was the research leads and the fresh lines of inquiry we were able to furnish to each other.

[16] As a result of his friendship with Dean Byron Cummings and to give him the benefit of an academic connection, Goodwin was named a research assistant of the Department of Anthropology of the University of Arizona.

April 4, 1932
Bylas, Arizona

Dear Opler,

I have both your letters here, and thanks a lot for the Chiricahua relative terms.

That's fine that they awarded you the fellowship, and I am glad to hear about it.

There has been quite a lot of talk about that murder trial, and I'm afraid Columbia is pretty unpopular out in the Southwest now, although I don't know just how much they are to blame for all this. Well, it's over and done now, anyway.[17]

I'm mighty glad to hear that you have started on your boundaries and will be interested to see how how they fit in.

In this letter are those place names in Chiricahua territory, the locations of which I am fairly positive of, and I listed them, as I thought you might want to have them when your friend is in Chicago.[18] The other names which I have, in Chiricahua territory, I know the approximate location of, but don't want to give them to you until I can give you their exact location. I hope you will be able to correlate your terms with these.

Also have sent you, under separate cover, twelve old photographs of my own, as the ones I ordered for you have not come yet. They are all Chiricahua, or Warm Springs, and I picked them mainly for the costumes shown. The costumes of the men are pretty typical of the Western Apache. That of the women is about the same also. I guess your friend will recognize a good many of the people. The titles to these pic-

-----

[17] During the summer of 1931 a graduate student in anthropology from Columbia University who was carrying on field work among the Western Apache was murdered by Indian youths. There was evidence that she had been extremely indiscreet, largely because of ignorance of how some of her actions would be construed. The trial and attending publicity dragged on until the spring of 1932 and made difficulties for those who wished to engage in Apache research during this period.

[18] A Chiricahua Apache was being brought to Chicago by the Department of Anthropology so that Harry Hoijer, the linguist, and I might continue work with him. During his stay I checked and amplified my Chiricahua notes and secured a still unpublished autobiography.

tures are incorrect in some instances, and these I have corrected as much as possible.

Now here is a thing that has been on my mind, and you may be able to give some idea about it. The Coyotero say that the Chiricahua and Warm Spgs. Apache and the other affiliated bands are more like the Mescalero in speech and certain customs. This seems to be borne out by your work last summer. I don't know how the Mescalero dressed or lived, but I should judge from what I've heard that externally they more resembled the Plains culture, is that right? Well, from what I can learn of the Chiricahua, etc., in external appearances they resembled the Western Apache more, and this you will see partly in these old photographs. I wish you would ask your friend whom the Chiricahua and Warm Spgs. Apache, and their related bands, considered themselves most closely related to in the old days — the Western Apache or the Mescalero. This is just a matter of curiosity on my part.[19]

Those terms "Pinal," "Pinal Coyotero," and "Pinaleño" are darned confusing, aren't they? And I think they're going to turn out not to be all separate bands. The Arivaipa, if any at all, more deserve the name of "Pinal," as the Pinal Mt. Range takes up a great part of what was their original range.

As to the Coyotero, here is the way I find them: they are all one people, and always were — that is, within the past 200 years or so — and are a very distinct people from the other three Western Apache divisions. The Coyotero were made up of three bands at the time the agencies were first set up, and these three bands were in existence before the agencies were put up, also. Each of these three bands had one headman, or chief. The way these bands were distinguished from one another was by the location of their farms, as they have been raising corn since before the agencies were put up. The westernmost band of Coyotero had all their farms on Cedar Creek (about 2 m. west of White River on your map). The middle band of Coyotero had all their farms at Canyon

---

[19] Goodwin's Western Apache informants were correct; in spite of a Plains orientation in dress and certain other traits, the Mescalero and Chiricahua were much closer to each other, linguistically and culturally, than either were to the Western Apache.

Day (just below the forks of White River, some 2 miles below Ft. Apache). The eastern band of Coyotero had their farms on the East Fork of White R., way above Ft. Apache, and also over at the Point of Pines, south of Black River, and at Eagle Creek (2 m. west of Point of Pines on your map). These farming places were considered home, and, from continually going back to them, the three bands began to be known to each other by three different names. However, they were always intermarrying, and it is confusing on this count. They also traveled around together, the three bands, or parts of them, mixed in. But each of the three bands generally had their own separate places where they went to gather mescal, juniper berries, or acorns, etc. These food-gathering camps lay to the south of the farming locations, clear down across the Gila River and south of it, in what I have marked on your map as Coyotero territory. The three bands, of course, went to those food-gathering camp sites which were nearest their farms, usually directly in a southerly direction. Because of this, it is hard to assign a separate territory to each of the three bands, and the best that can be done is to show the area over which each band usually went to gather its food. Really they (all three bands of Coyotero) considered the whole Coyotero area as sort of joint property between them. This is the way they were living up to the time the agencies were put up. Among the three Coyotero bands there were *nine distinct clans,* each clan with its own chief, who was more or less supposed to be under the chief for the whole band to which he belonged. This is the reason for so much confusion in the early records of the various chiefs and their bands.

After the agencies were set up, the three bands of Coyotero continued to hold their farms in the original places till about 1877 (not quite sure of the date, as haven't my notes here). In that year, due to certain troubles, the agent at San Carlos had them all move down onto the Gila River, under San Carlos jurisdiction, where all the other W. Apache peoples were being centralized. For a good many years (till about 1881, I think), they kept them down here, only letting them go back to plant and harvest their corn at the old farms. After this they allowed those Coyotero to move back for good to their old homes, around Ft. Apache. While on the Gila R.

the western Coyotero band were camped at Dewey Flats mainly, the middle band at Calva, and the eastern band at Bylas. Now all the people have moved back from Dewey Flats and Calva and are back around Ft. Apache, which is their real home. They are taken care of at the White River agency. A great many of the people moved back from Bylas, also, to their old home on East Fork and are taken care of at White Riv. agency. A good lot of them stayed on at Bylas, though, where they still are, and these are taken care of at the San Carlos agency. They are not a separate band, but only those Coyotero who did not choose to go back to their old homes. The people I am working with are all three bands of the Coyotero, which rightfully, it seems, should be treated as one people.[20]

I have some more answers to your questions in Chicago:

1. They played the game like baseball here also.
2. It was obligatory for a woman to marry her dead sister's husband, or, if not she, a close relative of her clan.
3. You can marry into your father's clan if the person you marry is not descended from your father's sister.
4. Adolescent girls use the scratcher and drinking tube.
5. The course of the hoop and pole game is not designated on one side by a color of any kind. But one pole always has its butt painted red, and the other plain.
6. They used to have a victory dance on the return from the warpath.
7. They still cut the children's hair in the spring, only for two successive years.

Here are some questions I would like you to ask your friend if it's not too much trouble:

1. Did his people use to trade and visit with the Navajo, Zuni, and Acoma?
2. Does he know of a band of people called the *nìndè•zn?* They used to travel around with the eastern band of Coyotero most of the time, but sometimes used to go and visit with the Chiricahua, to whom they were related.

---

[20] In his final version Goodwin recognized only two bands of the White Mt. group.

The Coyotero say that they are not the same as the *nìndà•i* (the outlaw Chiricahua band).[21]

3. Do his people have a term for older brother, older sister, or younger brother, younger sister?
4. Have they always used the sweat bath?
5. Did they use a sinew-backed bow?
6. Did they use the flute as a musical instrument?
7. Did they have any term for the equinoxes, or were they of any significance?

The following are the Chiricahua place names and their locations:[22]

1. *tudzà•né* (the "dz" is pronounced like "j" in "John." I put this in because there are a lot of "j" sounds like this, and "dz" is the one you gave me equivalent to it, but which is used otherwise in different words here, so I will indicate where it is given the "John" sound.)[23] This is the upper San Pedro Riv., in the vicinity of Fairbanks, Ariz.

2. *dzédàsa•* (with "John" sound). A hill right by Gleeson, Ariz., S. E. end of Dragoon Mts.

---

[21] The reference is to the Southern Chiricahua band. It became known as "the outlaw band" because many of the hostiles of the Geronimo campaign of 1885–1886 belonged to it. Geronimo himself was a member of this band.

[22] In the course of pacification or removal measures directed against the Chiricahua Apache, Western Apache scouts, usually in the company of friendly Chiricahua scouts, aided the United States military forces in the penetration of Chiricahua territory. In this way the Western Apache scouts learned what they claimed were Chiricahua names for places within the Chiricahua range, and Goodwin and I were trying to correlate the terms given to me by Chiricahua informants with the versions and descriptions obtained by Goodwin from the old Western Apache scouts. We found that there was a strong correlation, allowing for dialectical differences, between the use of the terms by members of the two tribes.

[23] That Goodwin did not employ separate symbols for the voiced alveolar affricative (then written "dz") and the voiced blade alveolar affricative (then written "dj")) was due to a misunderstanding. When I met Goodwin in Chicago, he was using a system of recording Apache words that he himself had devised. He asked me to acquaint him with the system which was in general use by American linguists and ethnologists, which has since been somewhat revised, and I sought to do this. Somehow the symbol for the voiced blade alveolar affricative was missed, with the resulting confusion. Goodwin was soon set right about the symbols to be used. Note that he was perfectly aware that two different sounds were involved.

3. *nàkíbitséè* = two his tails. Dos Cabezas Mt., Ariz.
4. *tsiyátà*. The Chiricahua Mts. in vicinity of Hilltop and Cochise Head.
5. *dziɬkisį·ke·ɬ*. A peak of the Mule Mts. at Bisbee, Ariz.
6. *ɣáinudzèe* (with "John" sound). San Juan Mt., in old Mex. just south of Naco, Ariz.
7. *dánàsdza*. Tombstone, Arizona, the hills there. ("John" sound).
8. *dziɬñjó*. Santa Rita Mts., Ariz.
9. *tséyadèdzula*. Rocky hills right by Ft. Bowie, Ariz.
10. *dziɬñdé·z*. The Peloncillo Mts., east of Ft. Bowie, Ariz., and from there running a long way south.
11. *kídècgij*. Janos, Chihuahua, Mex.
12. *tunte·ldzinlį* ("John" sound). Cave Creek, at its mouth, on west side of Chiricahua Mts.
13. *tudiɬhiɬ*. Douglas, Ariz.
14. *nadàzái*. The Mogollōn Mt., in New Mex., north of Silver City.
15. *tségǫte·l*. Near Reserve, New Mex., north end of Mogollōn Mt.
16. *túitcīhi*. The Rio Grande Riv., N. Mex.
17. *tsidahōlkai*. Cochise's stronghold, Dragoon Mts., Ariz.

There are 62 other place names of which I know the approximate location, which I will get exact before I send them on to you.

If there is any letter in your system that indicates the sound of "j" in "John," I would like to know it. Also how an "h" sound is indicated on the end of a syllable or word.

Hoping that you have a good time with your friend,

Sincerely,
GRENVILLE GOODWIN

April 15, 1932
Bylas, Arizona

Dear Opler,

Got your two letters today and also the letter with the Sapir system in it. Thanks a lot for it. It has made several things plain to me which I didn't understand about the system.

Glad the pictures got to you all right. They are my own, all right, but you are welcome to keep them as long as you want. When the ones I ordered come, I will trade with you, or you can just keep mine. However, you will probably want the new ones, as mine are a little worn.

Much obliged for answering my questions, and I was interested to hear your answer about the Chiricahua, or the three bands that constitute them.

The next place names I send will have their meanings written in. Sorry not to have done it the first time.

I guess that headdress must come from this region then, if your friend doesn't recognize it. So when I get the chance I will try and place it.

About Reagan, am sorry to say that some of the things he sets forth in his publication are decidedly cockeyed, as you probably have guessed.[24] The masked dancers I have never heard referred to as ghosts or ghost dancers, and I don't think Reagan ever did, either. The Coyotero term for them is *gá•n* or *łibáiyè* ("gray ones"); this is usually applied to the clown, who is also called *icdlé•jè* ("painted white"). The term for ghost or departed spirit is *t'cin*. They also use this now for our Christian devil. This must be what Reagan meant by his *cheden*.

The term of Reagan's, *gunelyiepa,* I have never heard of among these people. But it may easily be a term for some part of a sand painting, which he set down incorrectly, as all parts of a sand painting have their particular names. I can't tell you the exact colors as yet, but the most colors there

---

[24] The reference is to Albert B. Reagan, a government employee, who was more prolific than accurate in his writings on the Western Apache.

could be are red, green, yellow, black, and white. It is the same way with the figures. I can only tell you that they are in animal forms, sun, moon, etc., at the present time. I may be able to tell you more later on. The only term I know for a sand painting, meaning the whole thing, is *niɣéɣùtcí,* which is taken from the verb "to draw" or "paint," *gegùltcí.*

That's mighty interesting about your buffalo stories, but to be quite frank, I would be sort of skeptical. If you can, why don't you get an estimate as to how long ago this hunting occurred.[25]

I know that the Navajo did occasionally get over into the buffalo country and hunt buffalo, so it seems reasonable to suppose that the Chiricahua might also, but I'm positive they would have to go farther east for buffalo than the localities you describe. Here is my reason.

You almost never find any reference to buffalo ranging west of the Pecos River in New Mexico, and in the locality of Warm Springs, New Mex., I don't think buffalo were ever known. The flats nearest to the northeast of Albuquerque would be clear over the Sandia Mt., in the Estancia Valley. But no buffalo have ranged there within the past 300 years anyway, at the very least. There is an old saying among the Pueblo Indians of New Mexico that the buffalo never come west of the Pecos. The Coyotero knew what buffalo were, had a name for them, and owned a few buffalo robes, but these they obtained from traders. Their name for buffalo means a kind of blanket. But the Navajo name for buffalo alludes to the act of eating, which apparently shows they knew its meat. It would be interesting to know what the Chiricahua name for buffalo is.

The Coyotero are geographically and politically a distinct people from the rest of the Western Apache. They are also culturally distinct from the other three Western Apache groups in certain aspects, such as language dialect, versions of legends, some aspects of ceremonies, etc. This would hold true for each of the other three Western Apache groups as

---

[25] I had been told by a Chiricahua informant of a long journey to the northeast to hunt buffalo.

well. Each one of the four Western Apache groups considers itself a distinct people.

The Ft. McDowell Apache are really not Apache at all. They are called Mohave Apache also and were at one time held on the San Carlos Reservation. Culturally they are a lot like the Western Apache, in a material way, but it goes no deeper than this. They are really the same as the Yavapai and are a Yuman people, speaking a Yuman tongue. I have been on the McDowell Reservation a good many times, and it is easy to tell one of these people from a true Apache. Their features are much heavier than those of an Apache. The Yuma Apache are of the same stock as the Mohave Apache, but whether they are the same tribe or not, I do not know.

Here are some questions, if you have time for them:

1. What months do the Chiricahua especially set aside for storytelling?
2. Did they use saddlebags like the one whose picture I sent you?
3. Did they make bags out of whole hides of certain animals?
4. Did they use caps with antelope horns or cow horns on them?
5. Did they eat bear?
6. Did they use medicine buckskins, with ceremonial figures painted on them?

Glad to answer your questions, and can assure you I benefit from this correspondence as much as you.

Sincerely,
G. GOODWIN

May 14, 1933
17 Broadmoor Ave.
Colo. Spgs., Colo.

Dear Morrie,

Am writing to send you that book reference I told you about. It is *Official Correspondence of James S. Calhoun, While Indian Agent at Santa Fe, 1851–1857,* pub. by U.S. Dept. of Interior, Washington, D.C. This may not be the absolutely correct title, but you can find it by this, anyway.[26]

It was nice to see you again at Las Cruces and have a chance to talk. Sometime when things are a little further advanced, I want to get together with you and spend about a week just going over our material from A to Z and making comparisons so that what one of us has missed, the other may be able to give a lead on, etc.

I just completed my report and have sent it down to Tucson to be looked over and criticized. When it is free again, if you want to see it, I will send it on to you at Tularosa or wherever you are. However, they may keep it for quite a while down at Tucson, so can't say just when it will be free.

Thanks again for the photographs; they are very interesting ones to me.

Hoping your work is going well,

Yours,

GRENNIE

P.S. I'll be here for a few more weeks, but am going back to Arizona and work in June sometime.

Would like to trade my Las Cruces paper for yours!

---

[26] Goodwin and I had met again at an anthropological meeting at Las Cruces, New Mexico. He had told me about a book with a good deal of material about the Apache in it, which turned out to be Abel 1915.

May 22, 1933
Broadmoor Ave.
Colo. Spgs., Colo.

Dear Morrie,

Had your letter, and thanks for the paper. I have enclosed mine in return.

You certainly are a worker, what with all your plant and song gathering, etc., and I believe you have a greater daily capacity than I by a good ways, but we're both headed in the same direction, and I'll get to the goal some day, too.

What you said about the plants was interesting. Another thing that the Western Apache hold true is that the plants, all kinds, are the hair of Earth. Certain plants belong to Sun also, and such plants as these usually have no relations, but go by themselves. The sycamore is one of these. This tree is never struck by lightning and is almost like the head of trees, etc. Maybe you have somewhat the same conception at Mescalero. I sure want to see your plants sometime.[27] That's nice that you got a *gá·n* [masked dancer] outfit (I use the W. A. word). It will add greatly to the collection you already have.

Before you wrote I had not known of the accident that the fellows from Tucson had had. I certainly was sorry to hear about it and Dr. Provinse's ill luck.[28] It's pretty tough for him all right. I hope no one else was hurt.

The roasted mescal is pretty good, isn't it?[29] If you eat too much of the sticky part, it will give you diarrhea if you're not used to it. Anyway, it's good food. . . .

---

[27] I had gathered and pressed a large number of plants that were used by the Indians of the Mescalero Reservation for various purposes.

[28] John Provinse, chairman of the Department of Anthropology of the University of Arizona, had been in a rather serious automobile accident.

[29] The reference is to the crown of the agave, which was roasted in an underground oven. It is an Apache food staple.

Oct. 15, 1933
17 Broadmoor Ave.
Colo. Spgs., Colo.

Dear Morrie,

I have been all over your criticism and am accordingly writing you, taking up the points that you bring out in the same sequence.[30] Before starting, I had better explain that there is what I call my "question book," in which I write down questions and points that I want to ask or make more clear to myself in future field work. You have picked out several of these questions which I had in mind myself. In writing up the report, a good many questions and points concerning the social organization of the W. Apache came up which I wished to follow out before considering the report completed. As I have not had a chance to do this field work yet, I will have to put off the completion of the report until

---

[30] While I was engaged in field work at Mescalero, Goodwin had sent me the first version of his study of Western Apache social organization, with the request that I analyze it thoroughly and critically. I responded in a typed, eight-page letter of September 20, 1933. While I was warm in my praise of the manuscript as a whole, I called into question his reliance upon clan origin and migration legends as a guide to historical fact and indicated that I felt he had exaggerated the age and importance of the clan and the usefulness of his clan materials in clarifying the historical relations between the Western Apache and the Navajo. I also suggested that he provide a summary of the general nature of the economy so that the size and distribution of the social units could be better understood. I counseled that repetitious and technical materials, which would be boring to the general reader, be moved to appendices. I called certain ambiguities and errors to his attention and asked him to check on alleged Western Apache practices which seemed to depart from the general Apachean pattern. At the end of my letter I asked about the Apache Mansos, whom he had mentioned in his manuscript, about a plant which was in use in the burial rites of a religious cult at Mescalero which had had its origin among the Western Apache, and about Western Apache agricultural practices. Goodwin's early manuscript was premature, and though it was painful to have to carp at so much industry and achievement, at the time no one else commanded the field experience and comparative knowledge to call attention to many of the errors and defects. Goodwin defended a number of his positions with spirit in this letter, but an examination of pages 107–110 of his *The Social Organization of the Western Apache* (1942) will indicate the degree to which his treatment of the clan was ultimately modified. Most of my suggestions concerning arrangement and emphasis were also incorporated in subsequent drafts. Still, while other scholars also read the manuscript and no doubt gave helpful advice, none of our comments would have been worth much if Goodwin had not been able to provide such magnificent basic data.

such time as I can get back to Arizona again, which I hope will be sometime after New Years. But first off, thanks ever so much for your criticism.

I can see your point on the putting of the lists of chiefs and of some of the clan migration myths in the appendix. Also, your point about the discussion of the economy and subsistence is most helpful and one which I agree with you should be included in the discussion of social organization. Accordingly have written a brief account, about fifteen or twenty pages, which goes in very nicely at the end of the "Natural Environment" section of Part I. Of course, the detail is lacking in this, but detail will be taken up later on elsewhere, and I have plenty of most of it.

1. About use of sibling terms for great grandparents, am satisfied as to its general use among the Western Apache, though, of course, the practices of interrelation between such relatives is not often called into observance.

2. Return presents on part of bride's family; reciprocal feasts: Both these points were in use among W. Apache, though to a varying degree according to the station of the parents and family (wealth). However, the return presents of the bride's family were mainly a good will offering and not considered necessary, as were those of the boy's family. In poorer families probably hardly any presents, or none at all, would be given by the bride's family. Reciprocal feasts were often part of the affair, though they would be likely to be absent among poor people.

3. Sleeping at the husband's camp the first few nights: I know this was practiced among certain families, but I have it in my question book for further clarifying.

4. Hunt of man and wife after marriage = same as no. 3.

5. Headwoman: This was common to all W. Apache groups, and I can assure you it is not the overemphasized account of one person. However, the headwoman did almost always rise to her position without the choice of the people, but through her own accomplishments alone.

6. Man going back to his people at the death of his wife till his in-laws called to dispose of him: Am not sure quite what you mean here, but take it that you mean during his period of mourning. Men quite often choose to go back to

their close relatives, if they have any who will look after them, during this time. However, they may choose to stay with in-laws during this time and will most certainly do so if there is no other place to go. If I haven't got you right on this, let me know. At any rate, I will make more certain of this point than I am at the present time, when I go back to Ariz., that is, in which direction the majority of choices lie.

Page 7. About the choice of terms group, tribe, tribal group: I want to discuss them with you when we get together next time. If your tribe and my group are one and the same, I agree that the same term ought to be used for both.[31]

Page 7. My paper, I guess, was misleading on this point. What I meant was that the differences between W. Apache groups must have existed to some extent before the W. Apache became distributed in relation to each other as they were within historic times; that if they were all alike in the beginning of the historical distribution, all equally related, the differences could not have sprung up alone in their historical distribution in relation to each other.

Page 15. I mean bands here, but did not make it clear in what sort of situation. Accordingly it is changed now to "members of one band always live close to each other in the same big camp or group of camps when gathered together in any great number, especially at farming sites."

Page 71. I do not say that every Apache band is derived from the intermingling of clans, and most certainly the band is not derived from the growth of the clans. I merely say that *certain* bands among the W. Apache may be the result of the intermingling of clans which have lost their unity by migration and splitting up of their people in a new territory only insofar as migration traditions may be depended on.

Page 84. This is *only* applied to the W. Apache and to certain bands among them. The two principles that you say the data demonstrated to you are just the ones I was trying to bring out, only you have worded the idea very much better

---

[31] It was finally agreed that the group among the Western Apache was something more than a band and less than a tribe.

than I did.[32] I do not give these principles as generalizations here, but merely as demonstrated among certain bands of the Western Apache. The time for generalizations in reference to the whole Apache and Navajo people of the Southwest has not come yet, to my mind.

Page 120. I see your point here about using legends in an explanatory sense and have gone through the different places where they are used as such, indicating what I meant to in the first place and have overlooked, namely that these explanatory ideas based on legend are merely given at their face value and that said data, insofar as it is legendary, can only be taken in this way. However, these legends do bring out some very striking points from which interesting conjectures can be drawn and for which there seem to be no other explanations.

Page 134. I don't blame you for being puzzled, and the reason is a blunder on my part. The opening sentence now reads: "The structure upon which so much of the social organization of the Western Apache is built is the clan." The opening sentence about the local group stands as it is.

Page 134. As you probably noticed, the term "blood relationship" is used elsewhere in connection with clan. Your point is correct, of course, but nevertheless there is a *feeling* of blood relationship here, as the maternal clan relatives of an individual are not marriageable because they consider that the same blood flows in their veins as in his or hers.[33] The *feeling* has been indicated in the report since you read it to make the point clear.

Page 134. — 1. This is only applied to the Western Apache, not any other Apache.[34] In saying that the clan antedates the band and the group, I only mean that this is true within the present territory of the W. Apache. Before the W. Apache entered their historical territory, they may have

---

[32] I had objected to wording which seemed to imply that the Western Apache clans antedated band organization. The two principles of organization mentioned were kinship and locality.

[33] I had pointed out that since the clan was a unilateral kin concept, blood relationship was bound to exist with persons outside one's clan.

[34] I had asked seven specific questions about material which appeared in a paragraph on page 134 of his manuscript — hence these subordinate numbers.

had other prehistoric bands or groups, or they may not. This seems an impossible point to determine right now.

— 2. See first sentence in answer to question no. 1, p. 134.

— 3. It seems very probable that the local group is older than the clan among the W. Apache, judging from their historical social organization pattern, unless this pattern has undergone some unaccountable and great change, which last there seems no reason at the present time for believing.

— 4. This Las Cruces paper reference is not an explanation of the formation of a clan, but merely an explanation of the original nature of the clan among the W. Apache. However, I do believe that the local group may have been a nuclear factor in the starting of clans among both Navajo and W. Apache in certain cases.

— 5. "Time immemorial": your point agreed to. It is a bad expression to use. It was merely used in conjunction with the phrase, "back to the time when the W. Apache had not yet arrived in their historical territory."

— 6. In connection with clan migration stories and the possibility that the units now said to be clans were originally local groups and bilateral kin, I would say this. Granting the migration legends to be approximately correct, then if these prehistoric migrating people did not have the clan system at the time, it is also very probable that the Navajo, from whom they claim to have split off at that time, did not have the clan system, either. Then, after the two peoples had become separated, each develops a strong clan system, and this clan system of both peoples seems to be remarkably alike from what little I know of the Navajo. This change from a non-clan organization of the people to a strong clan system must have been derived by both Navajo and Western Apache from a common source, it seems reasonable to assume. (The source might be contact with a foreign tribe or tribes addicted to clans, it might be a marked change in mode of life of the people, or a combination of both these factors, etc.) Does it not seem more reasonable to say that the Western Apache — or at least the necessary amount of them (to contact the clan influence) — and the Navajo were probably together when they each received clan organizations, which today are so similar. Furthermore, when we know that the majority of Western Apache clans within historic times claimed relationship to certain Navajo clans and that most of the root clans claim that they came from north of the Little Colorado River, under their present names or legendary name, and that to this day corresponding clans of the same names are living north of the Little Colorado River among the Navajo, does the point not seem further made clear? Is it not choosing the long way round the mountain to say that the W. Apache and the Navajo each assumed the clan organization separately? If, then, we can suppose that the W. Apache and Navajo assumed the clan organization while together, then the W. Apache, when they migrated into their present territory and split off from the Navajo, must have already had the clan organization, and therefore the units described in the legends are very likely to be clans. For this idea there is, however, no material proof except the relations between Navajo and W. Apache clans within historic times and the corresponding together of certain W. Apache and Navajo clan names. It seems reasonable, though, to say that there must have been some reason for certain clan legends of the Western Apache, some movement of peoples on which they were based, no matter how exaggerated they may have become now. I will say, however, that I believe that there is a possibility that there were some Apache people already living within the territory of the W. Apache at the time the clans entered it. What the status of the clan was (if there was any clan at all) among such an Apache people as this (if there were such a people), it is impossible to say. I have no proof for the two preceding sentences, though, and merely offer it as one of many possibilities.

— 7. See answer to question 6.

Page 138. The description in the report does sound like the local group, I will admit, for I have failed to put in the fact that in the clan there were several chiefs. The whole clan as a unit among the W. Apache was far larger than the local group, as within it there were apt to be several local groups, each with its chief.

Page 149. What I meant was that the woman who used the clan design of her father's clan could not do so just because of her father's membership in the clan. To procure the right to use the clan design, she must have first cousins, children of her father's sister, to ask permission of. Her father or aunts and uncles (paternal) could not grant her the right. However, the reason for this is not quite clear to me yet, and I have it in my question book for further clarifying.

Page 257. Will leave this point about the value of legend till next we meet, when we can discuss it far better than we can on paper. Needless to say, your point about mythology being a rationalization is right, but there are other factors in the case which deserve some notice.

Page 295. The story about *dàsínè* was supposed to exemplify the heights a diligent girl might achieve to. The heroine in this case almost reached the station of a head-woman. However, maybe you are right and the point does not have enough relation to the story.

Page 393. Correction is right; should be "great grand-daughter." Thanks.

Page 473. The second-class in-law term *cìγį́‘* is not used commonly for the children of the wife's father's sister; this may be due to the fact that they are of the paternal clan, as you suggest. I am much interested in this point myself and do not understand it exactly. It is down in my question book for further inquiry. What is your special interest in this question and the one below?

Page 475. A woman's use of the second-class in-law term *cìγį́‘* does not exclude children of her husband's mother's brother, for the husband will call such cousins his brothers and sisters. Concerning its use in connection with children of the husband's father's sister, I have it down in the question book for further clarifying and in connection with the question above this one.

Page 475. What I meant by this was that all ordinarily third-class relatives-in-law make use of their third-class terms from time of marriage. The first- and second-class relatives-in-law, who may never observe the use of first- or second-class in-law usages, will nevertheless ordinarily observe the use of third-class terms from time of marriage likewise.

Page 490. My understanding of the case — and I am

pretty sure of it — is that between second-class in-laws, brothers and sisters of one's mate, polite form as well as avoidance could be terminated between members of the opposite sex, and that marriage could take place. However, I will put it down for further inquiry to be absolutely positive.

I don't know just who or what the Apache Mansos were. They were well known to the W. Apache but are now apparently extinct, or almost so, through intermarriage with Mexicans about Tucson. They were always friendly with the Mexicans and were employed by them a great deal as scouts against the W. Apache. The W. Apache say that they talked like Chiricahua, if that means anything. There are one or two families intermarried with Mexicans, said to be living in Tucson, and I have not been able to locate them yet, though I think I have a lead. However, the whole thing may turn out to be a wild goose chase. If anything turns up, I will let you know. Do you remember we talked about these people at Tularosa? I seem to recollect that Sam Kenoi had heard of them.[35]

About the use of the plant 'ĭyà'ą́į in burial ceremonies of S. J. Edwards, etc., among the W. Apache, I can't say.[36] I will put it down in the question book and let you know. The plant is common in the area of the W. Apache and formerly furnished food. There are two kinds distinguished by the W. Apache so far as I know.

Agriculture

Will first answer your ten questions.[37] There are quite a few of them which I do not know about but will inquire

---

[35] Goodwin had visited me in my home at Tularosa, New Mexico, just below the Mescalero Reservation. During his stay he had met and talked with a number of my Indian helpers, among them Sam Kenoi, a Chiricahua Apache.

[36] The plant I referred to was a sage, *Artemisia filifolius*.

[37] I had asked ten specific questions about Western Apache agriculture and had called for a general description of farming practices, besides. As his letter indicates, Goodwin obliged on both counts. Some of this material has been utilized, with full acknowledgements to Goodwin, in an article on certain comparative Apachean practices (Opler 1972).

fully into, as they will come naturally in the course of further field work. The results I will let you know as soon as possible.

1. About prayer sticks in the fields, can only say that I have heard the W.. Apache speak of the Navajo using them, but never of themselves doing so. They may do so.

2. In former times the *gá·n* ceremony was sometimes used to bring rain for crops, but my data are incomplete on this point, and I can't give you more information than this.

3. Cornmeal and corn pollen are used in certain ceremonies. Cornmeal is used as one of the four elements which go to make up the medicine that a girl is painted with at the puberty ceremony. This is to insure her having good crops of corn in the future, after she is married. I don't know of other uses, though there probably are some.

4. About corn fetish used: have never heard of it. It may exist among W. Apache.

5. About pregnant or menstruating women crossing fields: do not know. Very probably there is some rule about this.

6. Do not know of any grinding songs. They may exist. The metate is used often.

7. See question 3 answer. Also in the puberty ceremony complete corn plants (four) were planted about the ground of the ceremony at the cardinal points, and sometimes four corn plants were set up to the east of the ceremonial tipi. Beyond this I do not know of any agricultural products being used. The corn plants used must be complete: stalk, leaves, young ears, and tassels. As for the rest, data are not complete.

8. Among people of one local group, sometimes all families farmed, sometimes many families didn't farm. However, farming usually went by local groups, not by bands or groups. Thus the majority of families in one local group would own farms, or they wouldn't own farms. Of course, this did not always run true to form.

9. Land was usually inherited through the maternal line, that is, it stayed within the family group on the female side. However, I have more work to do on this point, and further points may come to light. Do not know of any strict rule in

inheritance of water rights, except that of priority of establishment of farming sites. The agriculture was really not
intensive enough in any one locality to give rise to disputes
over water rights, as it does among white and Mexican
farmers today.

10. Agriculture is reflected to quite an extent in the
mythology of the White Mt. group. Concerning other groups
it also exists in mythology, but to what extent I cannot say, as
I have not the full mythology of any of the other groups.

Agriculture of W. Apache

The crops raised were corn, squash, some beans, and
some wheat, which last was obtained from raiding Pima and
Mexican settlements. Corn was the biggest crop; beans were
not often raised. The beans were said to be gotten from Zuni,
and the White Mt. group seems to have raised them more
than other groups.

Fields were cleared of brush first, and any trees growing
on the plot, if they could not be burnt out right away, were
killed, and the lower branches were broken off to give room
for planting. Then a ditch was dug from the creek, sometimes from springs, to the plot. Men dug with digging sticks,
women carried off the dirt in baskets. All who were able
helped. Next a brush conversion dam was built across the
creek, if a creek was the water source, and both sexes again
worked, the women, of course, doing the lighter work, the
men lifting the heavy stones, etc. The work of building dam
and ditch was a community affair, because one ditch and
dam served several farms. Work on the farm itself, though,
is a family affair, and if more labor is needed than the family
can produce, this labor is hired, as you have already read in
the report (Part IV, "Family Group"). Both men and women
work on the fields, though usually there is a preponderance
of women when the work is light enough for them to man-
age it.

In planting, the field is first irrigated; then, when dried
off a little, it is dug up with digging sticks. Those digging
sticks were about three feet long, of hard, heavy wood, flat-
tened at one end and pointed. Now the ground was ready

44

to plant, and the women went along with a planting stick and punched holes in the ground, put seeds in, and covered them over. Planting depth was about 6 inches. After planting, the field was again irrigated two or three times at intervals. When the corn was up about 1½ ft., the people went off for the summer and left it to take care of itself, only leaving one or two people to keep animals out. Up to this time the corn was roughly weeded with a wooden hoe, later with iron hoes from Zuni trade.

In September the people returned and harvested the corn, and this took them up until the middle of Oct. usually. By that time the corn would be sorted over, some of it shelled, some left on the cob. All extra corn was stored away for future use in large ground caches, in caves, and in the wickiup at the farm. From then on many of the people remained at their farms the rest of the winter. In harvest, the work was done mostly by women and young boys and girls. Some men helped also.

This is a very brief description, but I hope it is what you want. When we meet next time, if there are any other things about agriculture that you want to know, we can talk about them. There is one more thing that I have omitted, and that is that snake medicine has a very definitive connection with corn crops. Men who have snake medicine are usually said to have good crops. My data are not complete on this last, though, as yet.

The size of average farms in old times would be about half an acre, or a little more or less (per family). Where dry farming could be practiced, irrigation was not used, of course.

Well, I hope I have answered at least some of your questions satisfactorily and that they may be of some help to you. I should judge that your intense interest in the agricultural complex of the W. Apache has something to do with your looking for a reason for the clan among the W. Apache. I would be glad to hear from you just what you are working towards, your ideas, etc., though I believe I can guess some of them.

If you get the time, write me a line, as would like to know what you are doing, or if you change your address, your

plans about Jicarilla, etc. Please don't think me too inquisi-
tive, but I just want to keep in touch with you, and somehow,
by hook or crook, I will make a point of seeing you before
I go back to Arizona again. Thanks again for the criticism.

Yours,

G. GOODWIN

Jan. 8, 1934
17 Broadmoor Ave.
Colo. Spgs., Colorado

Dear Morrie,

I thought that I would write you a letter today. I hope that you had a good Christmas and that the new year is a lucky one for you.

Things go on the same here for me, and I am still taking it easy, and putting most of my spare time in working up my notes and typing them, etc. It seems an endless job, but they are gradually getting done. Also spend a lot of time in reading.

How is your work progressing, and when do you think that you will be finished getting your material into shape at Tularosa? I hope that it is going well. Have you any idea yet as to what month you will be leaving the Mescalero country, and when you do leave there, will you be going right on to the Jicarilla, or what?

The reason that I ask you all these questions is that I want to keep in touch with your movements, so that at some time we can have that much-talked-of meeting together. You see, the way things stand with me, I won't be going back to work in Arizona till this summer sometime. My health is getting along fine, but it will be another five months before I will be completely on my feet again, and for this reason I am afraid that I will not be able to connect with you while you are still at Mescalero. However, after March I may be down in Santa Fe, and if you should come through on your way any place, we might meet there. But the truth of it is that right at the present time, even if it were possible for us to get together, either here or anywhere else, I would be of little use, as I cannot work for more than a couple of hours a day. However, you know that if you should be passing near the Springs here at any time, you are always welcome to stop here, and if nothing else, I could show you my Apache collection. I do not know for sure if I will even be in Santa Fe after March, but whether we meet there or not, I will look you up before going back to Arizona.

Am particularly sorry that I could not come down while you were still at Mescalero this winter, because there is one thing in particular that I wanted very much to talk over with you. This was concerning the remnant of the Apache people who are still running wild in Mexico. You will remember that we talked some of them before. I was wondering about how much information you had on them and if you were interested in them or not. You might know some of their relatives there among the Chiricahua at Mescalero, and if so, you might know of their attitude toward them, etc. The reason that I say this to you is that, as you know, I have been twice into Mexico to get information on them and am much interested in them. I have here a good deal of information concerning them, and I wanted to talk it all over with you. There appear to be some interesting divergences in house types which are very peculiar. I think that you would be interested in the data, and we will look it over sometime. Do you think that the Chiricahua at Mescalero would want to get into touch with these people and that they would like them to come back to the States and live with them on the reservation? There are a lot of questions like this that I would like to ask you. As far as I can find out, there are only about thirty men, women, and children left, roughly. They are fighting a losing battle in Mexico, and it seems only a question of time till they will be exterminated. In the last few years about five of them have been killed in fights with the Mexicans, and two of their girls have been captured by the Mexicans also. One of these girls is now grown and living at a town in Mexico. I heard that she wants to come back to her people on the reservation, if they are still alive. Last summer or spring, another little girl about eight years old was caught by two Mexicans. They kept her tied on the end of a rope that was fastened to a tree. A friend of mine down in Mexico offered a hundred pesos for her, but before he could get in touch with the Mexicans who had her, she had died. It is hard to imagine how wild these people are.

Well, there is lots more to tell you about all this, but we can do it better later on. The thing was that if you want to help me on this, it would be a fine thing if you could keep track of anything that you hear concerning these people. I would like to see something done about it, but just how it is to be done is the question. It is needless to add that anything concerning this subject that I tell you is in strict confidence.

This is about all that there is to write you of at the present time, and I don't know whether it will interest you or not. Please excuse this rotten typing, but I·am sitting outside, and my hands are cold and clumsy. The best of luck to you, and I will be hoping to hear from you when you get the time.

Yours sincerely,
G. GOODWIN

Jan., 1934
17 Broadmoor Ave.
Colo. Spgs., Colo.

Dear Morrie,

Was happy to get your long and very interesting letter and to hear about your plans and what you had been doing.

You must have a fine collection of plants and data on them. Also your mythology sounds very interesting. The sources of power and stories concerning them should be of greatest interest, and it is a thing that I have wanted to complete among the Western Apache for some time. However, mere writing is a waste of time here, as it does not express my intense interest in your results among the Chiricahua and Mescalero.

It is fine that you are going on with the Jicarilla work, and I only hope that you succeed in making as successful a study of these people as you have of the two peoples you have already surveyed. This also goes for the Lipan as well. Won't it be a grand thing when we have the complete surveys of Chiricahua, Mescalero, Lipan, Jicarilla, and Western Apache and can lay them down side by side, with all their similarities and divergences apparent?

About the Apache in Old Mexico we can talk later. Can only say here that at present it would be utterly impossible to get anyone to represent them, as you suggest. In view of this, I wouldn't approach the Mescalero agent, would you (at least, not at present)?

I guess you forgot to say in your letter just which numbers of the *Jl. Amer. F-1* or *American Anthropologist* you wanted. But it doesn't matter because I have no old numbers of either here. I have some numbers of both, but only for the last two or three years. However, if there are any of these that you want, would be glad to loan them to you. I don't know whether the Laboratory at Santa Fe has any of what you want. They might have.

About the questions you raise about the effect of agriculture on other aspects of W. Apache culture: there are some of these questions which you asked me before, in your criticism of my report, you remember. These are, namely, use of plants in ceremonies and reference in mythology to agriculture. But will say here that there are certain White Mt. myths, parts of which have to do with the procuring of corn from Turkey, and there are passages in these myths which tell of crops being planted. But these mythological references to agriculture are not of a religious or ceremonial character. They are mainly commonplace references showing that the people planted some crops. If you still have my letter about these things, then you will see the answers to these questions as best I am able to give them at present, but if my letter is gone, then will write you again if you will let me know. There are no myths the whole of which have to do with agriculture or agricultural products.

I enclose a brief discussion of the material side of the economic life of the W. Apache. It is the one which goes in my report, so will you please save it for me, or send it back when you get through with it. However, keep it as long as you like, as I do not need it now. You will see in this paper that I have not attempted to show how (the reasons why) the social organization of the W. Apache may have adapted itself to the economic life, but merely what economic life the W. Apache had to exist on. Its effects on the social organization and culture of the people, I want to take up fully, later on, in another paper. So I hope you will not be disappointed with the present discussion here enclosed, as I realize its deficiencies.[38]

Your other questions I will answer now as best I can. I think that instead of answering your questions right out, it would be better if I just gave a brief discussion covering your questions as best I can. As I have told you before, my material on many aspects of W. Apache culture is scanty, and so I cannot give you all the information on your questions that I would like to just now. However, these blanks will all be

---

[38] I had urged Goodwin to show the interrelations between the economic and social life of the Western Apache, to trace the reflections of agriculture in all other aspects of the culture, and to use Northern Tonto bands which did not engage in agriculture as a control in estimating the effects of agricultural practices. In response, he had written and enclosed a manuscript which was later published as Goodwin 1935.

filled out in further work when I go back, I hope, and when this is done your questions can be answered more fully. I believe that some of your questions are taken care of in the enclosed paper, so will not repeat them here.

The reflection of agriculture upon other aspects of the W. Apache culture is not a major quantity, when compared with that of game or wild plant foods, etc. Agriculture was not depended on as much as the other two sources of food. Therefore its effect on parts of the culture in many ways seems negligible at present. Agricultural products were not bartered to any extent, except when one family traded with another family who had corn. The first family would trade wild food products for the corn most likely. However, a real barter for corn did exist between certain Western Apache peoples and the Zuni and Hopi, in which baskets, etc., were traded to get corn. There is nothing so accentuated with the W. Apache as the corn complex is among the Navajo and Pueblo peoples. In most ceremonies corn or other agricultural plants do not play nearly the part that wild plants, etc., do. In ceremonial drawings the motifs are more often animals and people. In basketry the designs are usually geometric and have nothing to do with agriculture so far as I know. However, occasionally a cornstalk is used in decoration. But there is nothing approaching the use of agricultural products in design or ceremony that exists among the Navajo.

About the order [of importance] of domesticated and wild plants in songs, I cannot say at present. The point you bring up is a most interesting one. The most important ceremonies among the Western Apache do not have to do with agriculture, but rather are directed toward the benefit of an individual or individuals in curing, sickness, puberty, war, etc. There is no concerted agricultural ceremony by all the people of a community, as among the Pueblo peoples. Instead, where there is ceremony connected with agriculture, it is more of an individual relation — that is, the owner of the crop has to look out for the ceremonial side of the situation himself. It is very much the same as a man who has deer medicine power. A man who has this deer medicine power is almost always said to be successful in hunting deer or in making other men kill deer (bringing them the chance to do so). A man who has snake medicine power, among the White Mt. people, is usually considered to be able to produce good crops. Do you see what I mean? Agricultural power or medicine, success of crops, rests more on the individual than on a concerted action by the people in importuning some deity or deities, or rain, etc., to come and help them. It fits in with the general scheme of individual holy power or medicine power as I now understand it among the W. A. If what I say proves to be true, it ought to be of some interest, don't you think? I am looking forward a great deal to working all this complex out soon. In ending, I would like to point out that agriculture among some of the Western Apache was almost considered a luxury; that is, agriculture was not an integral part of their culture, and they could easily get along without it if they had to, as in all parts of the W. A. territory there were a sufficient variety of wild plants growing and game on which they could sustain themselves alone. Thus there were local groups living contiguous to each other, some of which planted, some of which didn't. This was true in almost all the different bands.

About the population of the W. Apache before the whites came into the picture (1860 roughly), it is a pretty risky thing to name a figure. At this time I would say that the W. Apache numbered from 6,000 to 8,000 souls all together. However, this is a very rough guess, and the figure may be well under this. It is above 4,000, though, I am sure, and possibly above 8,000. The Northern Tonto group is the one you mean when you say the group that didn't practice agriculture. But there were only two bands, out of the four bands in the group, which did not practice agriculture. The two nonagricultural bands had so much intercourse with the other bands which did practice agriculture that it seems improbable that there will be any great differences due to agriculture or lack of it. The Northern Tonto were the smallest in numbers of population, but this is the group which was mixed with the Yavapai, if you remember my report, and therefore, with Yavapai added, the population comes up considerably. There is no staple diet which would form a substitute for agriculture in the territory of the two non-agricultural bands which does not exist in the territory of agricultural bands in equal quantity. However, these nonagricultural bands lived in territories with few agricultural sites and were far more exposed to enemy attacks (see enclosed economic discussion). They did trade for agricultural products, but not to excess. They did not depend on domestic foods to any degree. Their clan system so far has proved to be just as strong and of the same pattern as that of agricultural bands. There was not enough economic difference between the subsistence of nonagricultural bands and agricultural bands to produce a marked difference in social structure, though minor differences in culture may come to light later on in the work. Well, all this is a point which interests me as much as it does you, and later on we will be able to discuss it to better advantage, I hope. You understand that all this and the discussion of agricultural reflections in the culture of the people preceeding it are my present reactions, which may change in the course of further investigation.

You probably know as much as I do, if not more, about the state of agriculture among the Navajo before they took up stock-raising, so will not discuss it here. But I can tell you something of the state of agriculture among them at the present time, though I don't know of how much value it will be. Among the Navajo as a whole, agriculture (corn, squash, melons) is an important institution, as you know. Throughout the Navajo country there are some families who do not practice agriculture but exist on stock-raising, etc., but these are almost always people who do not farm because they lack the facilities (sites, water). If there is any available site, a Navajo will put in a little patch of corn. These farms vary in size from a quarter of an acre to two acres, or perhaps more. Most of the crops are raised by dry farming, though along the San Juan there are large Navajo farms which are irrigated from the river. But due to the intense aridity of the Navajo country, the people have to depend on enough rain during the summer to bring their crops through. The religious side of agriculture, as you know, is marked and very similar to the Pueblo usages in many ways. In design, etc., it also appears. Those families who do not have their own farms usually procure corn, etc., from relatives or others who do have farms. Well, you probably know all this already.

What seems of great interest and importance in the comparison between the agriculture of the Western Apache and the Navajo is this: the difference between the country of the Navajo and that of the W. Apache is extreme, and therefore the natural obstacles and environment that the two peoples have to cope with differ greatly, and much of the economic basis is shifted. The Navajo country throughout is practically identical in nature with that of the Pueblo peoples. There is intense aridity, great dependence on rain for crops, scarcity of game, and only a few of the wild plant foods that exist in the W. Apache country and that of the peoples among whom you are working. The Navajo has to plant deep in the ground like the Pueblo, he has to pray hard to get rain like the Pueblo, for if there is no rain, then he is out of luck, as he generally depends on it alone. If his crops fail, he cannot fall back on the great variety of wild plant foods that the W. Apache has. So, you see, it puts him practically in the same boat with the Pueblo peoples when it comes to agriculture and the culture connected with it. The situation of the W. Apache is far different from all this, as you can see. He lives in a country where rainfall is more common, or if there is no rain he always has many streams and springs to irrigate from, etc. He does not have to plant deep in the ground, and there is not the great ceremonial, as well as physical, effort which the Navajo has to put forth to implore or demand help from heaven that his crops may mature. In a slangy way, "it comes easier" to the W. Apache, and there is not the concentration on the problem that the Navajo give it. Well, I don't know whether all this is of much interest to you, so I will quit.

Your letter has just come telling about the old Mex. Apache, and I was very interested to get it.[39] It almost makes me wild to have to sit at home like I do, but never mind. I'll be on the way soon. The stories you give about the Old Mex. Apache are very interesting to me, and the list of people will be no end of help. But don't get the expectations of your

---

[39] Some of the Apache at Mescalero were sure that certain of their relatives had survived the Indian wars and were, with their descendants, still in Old Mexico.

friends up for a safe return of these people, at least so far as I will be of any help. If it ever goes through, it will be a process of several years, don't you think? So don't lead your friends to expect anything, will you? There is too much of the wild goose chase about the whole thing to put any dependence on results.

Will say here that it would be utterly impossible to get any white man or Mexican who could get in touch with these people. They are too wild, and it would be like trying to get into touch with a pack of wolves. They have absolutely no contact with any people outside themselves that I know of. My own friends, the W. Apache, are scared to death of them and have no contact. It may be possible to act through the girl in the Mexican village, though I don't know. She has been so long away that it may be impossible to get her to help. These people are only rarely seen by Mexicans and whites, and then only by accident. They live back in the Sierra Madre, and if you had been down there, you would understand how inaccessible they are. I have thought about it a lot, and what you say about taking an old timer down there seems to me the only way of getting any results, even if this is possible. But we can talk it over later, and I want you to see some of the material that I have which was taken from a camp of these people. The only thing is that I won't be able to help in any way for a year or so, and there is not a soul in Mexico whom I know that could help. It may be possible to get in touch with the Apache girl by mail, and I will try it sometime. But I just wanted to let you know that it will all take a long time, a very long time, so don't get your friends steamed up for immediate action, will you? When we get together this summer, we can put all the odds and ends that we have on the subject together and see what they come to. Will let you know when I will be in Santa Fe, and in the meantime if I can give you any information about the Old Mex. Apache or W. Apache (comparisons with Mes. and Chir.), let me know.

Sincerely,
G. GOODWIN

P.S. Don't let my discussion of agriculture lead you to think that I don't believe there are any reflections from agriculture on other aspects of the W. Apache culture. I know that the reflections exist, and I will be on the lookout for more of them in further work. The discussion here is just a very superficial one.

Feb. 2, 1934
17 Broadmoor Ave.
Colo. Spgs., Colo.

Dear Morrie,

Your letter reached me safely. There is no hurry about returning the section about the economic life of the W. Apache, so keep it as long as you have need for it. On second thought, I guess that mesquite beans and piñon nuts could be added to the list of important plant foods. The W. Apache still use both, just as your friends do.

You are getting to be a real Apache, doing everything four times, and hereafter I will be prepared. I do the same way myself, so have nothing to talk about.

I am sure there is a reason why snake medicine is connected with the ability to raise good crops, and I think that later on it will be fully explainable. However, at the present time I do not have this information, so cannot give it to you. The one thing I do know about the point is that in mythology the pollenation of the corn plants in the fields was a time when the snakes came to the field in great numbers, because they liked to get the corn pollen. Therefore one of the connections of snake medicine with corn crops runs probably along this line, or others similar to it.

At the present time the Navajo live scattered out over the whole reservation far more than the W. Apache do. The need for finding good grazing for their flocks would keep them on the move more than the W. Apache. Therefore I guess they are probably more nomadic at the present time. But from what I have heard about the old times, it would seem that the W. Apache were somewhat more nomadic than the Navajo because of their making the practice, as you know, of following the wild harvests from one locality to another. The Navajo, of course, had to lead a nomadic life also, on account of their flocks. But the Navajo moved about mainly to obtain good grazing, whereas the W. Apache went from place to place for a rather different reason. The old Navajo local group pattern, however, much resembled the old-time local group of the W. Apache, as far as I know.

There are two main types of dwelling among the W.

Apache, though other minor types do exist. Below is an outline of the two main types. [See fig. 2.] I have drawn no. 2 the same height as no. 1, but it should be lower. They are both about the same diameter. The diameter varies from 12 ft. to 20 or 25 sometimes, on the floor, but usually averages 15 to 18 ft. roughly (I don't have the exact measurements here at the moment, and this is not exact). The height of no. 1 is from 7 to 15 or 18 feet roughly, according to the size of the diameter at the bottom. The height of no. 2 is usually not over 7 or 9 ft. Both no. 1 and no. 2 have a round floor plan, with the fireplace in the center. No. 1 can either have a covered entrance, as shown, or often does not have one. No. 2 usually does not have a covered entrance, though sometimes it does. Both have doors of wood on hinges now, but in the old days a door cover of thick boughs laced together was usually used. Both are covered first with several layers of grass thatching, and then over this is a layer of bear grass thatching, almost like shingling, in a way. In the low country where bear grass cannot be obtained, a layer of river willow branches is laid on the frame, and over this a layer of grasses or a layer of dry cornstalks laid close together. All thatching is tied securely on the frame in bundles, with yucca strands. Neither type has a smoke hole usually, though in summer a vent is sometimes made at the top of the dwelling. Nowadays over the thatching is tied a big canvas tarpaulin to aid in waterproofing. In summertime much of the thatching is removed to let cool air inside. The difference, as you can see, lies in the frame of the two types. [See fig. 3.] In no. 1 the poles are set in the ground with the bent side out and are fastened together at the top. In no. 2 the poles are set in the ground and bent over so that their tips meet and run parallel to each other. Then they are lashed together in this way. Both types have the binding sticks running around from pole to pole on the sides. This is just a rough description, but I think you will be able to get an idea from it. If you want more particulars, let me know.

About the N. Tonto use of corn products you mention in connection with the girl's ceremony, I can't say, as I haven't gotten that far yet. The same applies to their use of pottery.

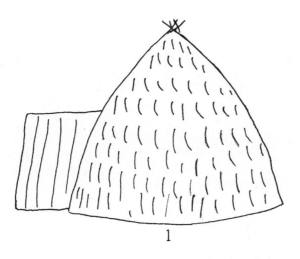

1

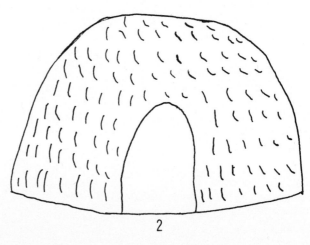

2

[Fig. 2. Main Western Apache house types]

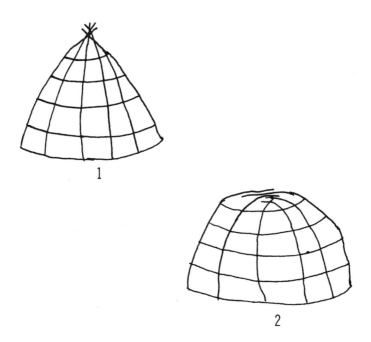

1

2

[Fig. 3. Differences in house frames]

Was interested to hear what you had to say in connection with the Apache in Mexico, and even if someone else does do something before we get a chance to, it won't stop our interest in the matter, do you think? I am looking forward greatly to talking it all over with you.

Well, I hope your work continues well.

Yours sincerely,

G. GOODWIN

Feb. 19, 1934
17 Broadmoor Ave.
Colo. Spgs., Colo.

Dear Morrie,

Thanks for sending back the economy section, and I am glad that you liked it.

About the house type that Blumensohn described to you with the gable roof, at White River, I am sure that he means the same type that I have seen.[40] However, as far as I can find out, it is not a very old type, not more than about forty years, and even now it is not often seen. About the Western Apache dwellings being more substantial than those of the Chiricahua, I can't say, as I don't think that I have ever seen a real dwelling of the latter people. The ones that the very few Chiricahua live in who remain among the Western Apache are just the same as those of the latter people. But I guess that this doesn't go to prove anything, as they are all intermarried with Western Apache now and have been for a long time. Those Chiricahua dwellings which I have seen in Mexico are so radically different from any other Apache dwelling that I can imagine, that I cannot believe them to be the original type that I have heard you describe.

About sun-baked, unfired pottery: outside of those toys made by the children, have never heard of this among the Western Apache. All their pottery was fired.

About the one who takes the part of *łibaye* among the Mescalero: have never heard.[41] The nearest thing that I know of to what you describe is the term sometimes given to *łibaye* of *'icdle•je* ("painted white"), but this is apparently not the same thing that you have.

The close comparison that you are making with the Navajo data sounds most interesting. I am also reading up

---

[40] Jules Blumensohn had visited White River in the late summer of 1931 in order to gather material about a modern religious cult started by Silas John Edwards, a Western Apache. By this time the cult had spread to Mescalero, where the members of the summer field party of the Laboratory of Anthropology had encountered it.

[41] Mescalero Apache informants had described to me a special type of masked dancer, Blackened One, who sometimes replaced the clown but had much more serious functions.

on the Navajo and Pueblo cultures to the north of the W. Apache and the Yuman peoples to the west, in order to get some pointers in a rough comparison of cultures. It has been most interesting. I didn't learn anything of the long chants or the gods you speak of while in the Navajo country, but what you say about the so-called "gods" resembling the personifications of powers as you have found them among the people you have studied seems to me to be a very reasonable idea. There seems to have grown up a very conventional terminology about the Navajo and their religion which is applied to them alone but which, if put in more straightforward and up-to-date words, would be applicable to the corresponding Apache usages much more so than it is now, don't you think so? So far as I now know, there are no gods among the W. Apache such as the *xǫ·ct'cin,* and the ceremonies are not anywhere near so formalized among all the forms as are the Navajo ones. But I can see how, if the W. Apache ceremonies should become very much more formalized and conventional, they would far more resemble those of the Navajo. Well, all this doesn't lead much of anywhere, and so I will close. One more thing that I have often thought about is whether the *gá·n* of the W. Apache are akin to the so-called "gods" of the Navajo.[42] There seems some reason to believe that there is a little likeness of the two, and I wonder if this is also true of the Mescalero and the Chiricahua.

As ever,
G. GOODWIN

---

[42] Goodwin is calling attention to the resemblances between the masked dancers of the Western Apache and the "gods" of the Navajo, a comparison that is certainly valid.

Sept. 5, 1934
c/o W. L. Goodwin, Jr.
P.O. Box 282
Santa Fe, New Mex.

Dear Morrie,

I was much interested to get your letter, but it was rather sad to hear of the death of so many of the old timers down at Mescalero. However, I guess that it is inevitable.

Of course you are welcome to one of the *gá•n* pictures if you want one.

Your findings on the social organization of the Jicarilla sound most interesting, and from what you say in your letter there seems to be a strong similarity to the Navajo system in some respects.[43] Last winter I went over the Navajo material available carefully and in it found the joking relationship between grandchild and grandparent that you mention and also that between an individual and certain members of his parents' generation. I have a long list of similar leads from the Navajo, etc., which I am most anxious to follow out when back at work. Am sending you that part of my paper which you wanted to borrow, and hope that there may be some leads in it for you in your Jicarilla work and that it will be otherwise useful. Very probably there are a number of social organization points lacking in it, which on further investigation might be found in the W. Apache system, and any leads that you can give me either from the Jicarilla or the Chiricahua and Mescalero will be greatly appreciated. The more I look at that MS of mine on the social organization, the more I realize that it will have to be rewritten. What material there is in it is sound all right, but I want to get at it and write some of the parts over again and fill in the gaps on the data. The errors in the recording of the Apache words, of course, will have to be corrected also, but that will not be so hard to do now, thanks to Hoijer. There is no hurry about returning the paper, so keep it till you are through with using it.

---

[43] By this time I was working on the Jicarilla Reservation and was giving Goodwin a first report of my findings. Immediately before the initiation of my Jicarilla work I had visited Goodwin at Santa Fe.

I know that you are up to your ears in work, but if you have the opportunity sometime there is something that I wish you could do for me. I would like very much to have a brief description of the main social divisions of the Central Apache;[44] that is, a description of the structure of the units you term "tribe," "band," and "local group," and what constitutes them. In connection with the local group, how large was it generally? Was there only one chief in it, or were there several? Was one band made up of several local groups? How much difference was there in culture between the bands? Did they have any difficulty in understanding each other's dialects? Did all the families of a local group stick together generally during the whole year and form a community, or were there definite subgroups within the local group which formed self-sufficient units by themselves and lived far apart from each other? Please don't bother to answer any of the above at any length, but, you see, I would like to have a little better understanding of the situation than I do, the Central Apache being the neighbors of the W. Apache. I know we talked quite a lot on the subject when you were here, but it would be of great help to me to have it in black and white, where I can see it. However, there is no rush about it at all, so don't bother till it is convenient.

There is one more thing: could you draw a rough diagram of the Central Apache, showing the three bands and the subdivisions or local groups within the three bands? Don't bother to put in rivers or mts., etc., but if you could, I would like to know the Apache names for the bands and local groups on the map. But please don't trouble about accuracy, just make it a mere sketch.

I want to get the Central Apache outlay straight, so that I can compare it with that of the W. Apache. Until we talked down here, I had always thought that you called each of the three bands of the Central Apache a tribe, and thus I compared what you really called bands to what I called groups among the W. Apache, so you can see that it was rather a sur-

---

[44] By "Central Apache" Goodwin is referring to the Chiricahua Apache.

prise to me when you said that the Apache in toto were divided into nine tribes—three tribes constituting the Eastern Apache, one tribe the Central Apache, and five tribes the Western Apache. Am not sure that I have quoted you right, but I think that's what you said. Concerning the W. Apache, I have always thought of them as constituting a single tribe (as per the above classification), just as the Mescalero or the Jicarilla do. So far as I know, the Northern Tonto are the only people among the W. Apache who might possibly be classed as a separate tribe from the rest of the W. Apache, as generally, outside of minor differences, the culture of all W. Apache groups is much the same. Well, the point is not very important right now, and we can talk it over better later on sometime, but I did want to let you know that this was my concept of it.[45]

It was nice seeing you and your wife here, and I enjoyed talking shop with you a great deal. I hope that you may get down this way again, and if you do, please remember to come out and see us again. Well, best of luck in your work, and I hope that you accomplish a great deal, even if the Jicarilla social organization does make you dizzy. Will be much interested to hear your results.

Yours sincerely,
GRENVILLE GOODWIN

---

[45] It is now generally agreed that there are seven Apachean-speaking tribes: Chiricahua, Jicarilla, Kiowa Apache, Lipan, Mescalero, Navajo, and Western Apache.

June 2, 1935
Bylas, Arizona

Dear Morrie,

Thanks a lot for sending on the paper and the reprint. I have read both and am returning the paper to you in this envelope. I enjoyed reading it a lot and found it interesting. The comparison of the Jicarilla culture with that of the Chiricahua was certainly illustrative of your point.

Much obliged for the reprint. Have read it through, and there are things in it which were of value to me. Am sending you in this cover a reprint of my paper in the *Anthropologist* in return, though you probably have the issue of the magazine.

It would certainly be nice to see the summary of the Jicarilla culture that you speak of, and if you get hold of a copy of it at any time and can spare it, I would certainly appreciate the loan of it.

There is no hurry about the rough map of the Chiricahua territories, and if you are going to work your data on these points out further, it will be fine.

My work is coming along, and I have accomplished quite a lot. There are a lot of new things that have come up, at least new among the W. Apache, and some of them are mighty interesting to me, and I think that they would interest you also. But probably you already have many of them among your own data from the Jicarilla, Chiricahua, and Mescalero. Many of them have to do with things that seem to apply more to the W. Apache than the Chiricahua and Mescalero, such as agriculture and clans, so I don't know if they would be of value to you right now.

There is one thing that is rather interesting which has come up in the social organization line, and I wonder if you have run across it in your work. It is this: a youth or man is sometimes "framed" by a girl's family, so that he will lose some of his property. The girl or young divorcée or widow will make up to a man in such a way that he will think she cares for him. After a while he may try to become familiar with her and touch her. If he does, she will go and tell her people, and they will go and kill a horse belonging to the man and eat it, or take some other property from him. This is, of course, the regular procedure when a thing of this kind happens under normal circumstances. Payment for damages of all kinds (injuries, etc.) is common among the W. Apache, and I have a lot of data on this sort of thing, but this was the first time the above turned up. It is sort of like our "Broadway gold diggers," isn't it?

I hope that your work is coming along successfully.

Sincerely,
G. GOODWIN

P.S. If anything more turns up of interest in my work here, I'll let you know. One thing more I have just thought of. In old times a man would ask some maternal relative to watch the actions of his wife while he was absent, and see if she went astray. A report was made to the husband unbeknownst to anyone else on his return. Have you run across this? There is a term to designate this.

July 11, 1935
Bylas, Arizona

Dear Morrie,

Was much interested to get your letter and to hear how the Lipan work was turning out.[46] Your results are certainly leaning toward something new in the way of cultural affiliation among the Apache tribes concerned, and I will be looking forward to your final summing up of the relation among the Lipan, Jicarilla, and Kiowa Apache, and to Harry Hoijer's linguistic work this summer. The lack of any avoidance of relatives by affinity is rather a shock, isn't it?

The reference to a joking relationship between grandparents and grandchildren among the Navajo is in Reichard's *Social Life of the Navajo Indians,* so I don't know how dependable it is. However, if you want to look it up, it is on pages 73 and 88. There are so many things in this book that look fishy to me that I hesitate to take anything too seriously in it, but you can take it for what it is worth.

As far as the material that you saw on the social organization of the W. Apache in my MS goes, it is still all right in general outline. There are some points that will have to be radically changed in view of later work this spring and summer, but these are not many. However, there are a lot of new things that have cropped up which I overlooked before and which will have to be fitted into the scheme. They do not change the data in my social organization MS so much. It is just that they make it a lot more complicated in its structure. There are a lot of interesting things come to light.

Now to answer your questions as best I can:

1. The self-reciprocal kinship terminology still stands, exactly the same. You remember that you asked me one time if the father's brother and mother's sister were not called by parent terms, as would be natural to suppose in the case

---

[46] I had completed my Jicarilla field study and had returned to Mescalero to work with the Lipan, who shared the reservation with the Mescalero and Chiricahua. A number of unexpected Lipan cultural features had shown up, such as the absence of avoidance and formal speech usages between relatives-in-law, although such usages had been prominent among the Apache groups I had investigated to this point.

of a clan organization. Among the White Mt. group they are definitely not, nor do such siblings of the parents use terms for ego that the parents would. There is an indication that they do this among the Tonto, but I have not worked this out definitely yet. The Navajo do it, according to the literature on them, but from this same literature I understand that in almost every case where it occurs there is also an obsolete term or one used in certain districts, not generally, that is the same as the equivalent W. Apache term. From what I can find out, the Navajo kinship terminology, outside the above usages, is about the same as the W. Apache one. The usage mentioned above for certain Tonto is not the prevalent one for the Tonto; it just occurs there.

2. The W. Apache use the terms *size• de* and *ciłna'ac* for the children of brothers of the mother, whether an actual brother or not, and also for children of sisters of the father, whether actual sisters or not.[47] There is no avoidance between any of these to the extent of not being able to see each other. Such an avoidance is unheard of. However, with such cousins who are closely related to you by blood you have to act almost as you would with a blood brother or sister — you cannot joke with them or wrestle with them, etc. But with cousins of this same class who are not closely related to you by blood there are two ways in which you can behave — you can either treat them as you do the closely related blood cousins of this class, with a little less formality, or you can have a joking relationship with them which entails all sorts of horseplay and joking. The sister or parallel cousin is more respected and you are more formal with her when she is of the opposite sex than you are with the cross-cousin of the opposite sex. "This is because she is more closely related to you," the W. Apache say. I don't know just how far the avoidance between cross-cousins goes among the Apache you have worked with. If it extends to not being able to see each other, there apparently is a difference between the W. Apache and your friends, as

[47] These were also the Jicarilla terms for cross-cousins; joking and restraint relations, according to sex, existed between Jicarilla cross-cousins. I was seeking to obtain comparative materials on this and other special kin usages from Goodwin.

over here not being able to see your cross-cousin is astonishing. Would be much interested to hear about the avoidances between cross-cousins that you have found.

3. With the father's blood brothers and sisters and anyone he calls brother or sister, whether related by blood or not (such kin are all grouped together), there is no joking relationship. You treat them all alike, with respect, as you would your father. There is no special relationship with them outside the one of occasional gifts and help to each other. Their behavior to you is the same, also. Blood brothers and sisters to your father by the same parents are considered helpful relatives that you can rely on in time of need, but not to the extent that your mother's brothers and sisters by the same parents are. Your mother's blood brother is really the closest relative you have in the first ascending generation, and likewise your sister's sons play the same part to you in the first descending generation. With blood brothers of your mother or with anyone she calls brother (these kin are all grouped together), there is no continual joking relation. You treat them with respect, and they you, though there are no polite terms or anything like that used. However, occasionally individuals do joke with such brothers to their mother, and they joke back as well, but this is only done with distant brothers to the mother, never with close ones. Am not fully satisfied about this joking relationship yet, and so for the time will call it not regular, but just something that occurs rarely and is more of an individual trait. Exactly the same thing is true of blood sisters of your mother or anyone whom she calls sister. Later on, when I am certain of this, I will let you know. It may turn out, after all, to be a regular joking relationship.

4. The children of siblings or cousins of the same sex as you, you call by different terms from those used for the children of siblings or cousins of the opposite sex. Thus a man calls children of siblings or cousins of the same sex as he *"cibe•je,"* of opposite sex to him *"cida'a";* and a woman calls children of siblings or cousins of the same sex as she *"cika'a,"* and of opposite sex *"cibe•je."*

5. Between you and your mother's parents or their siblings (these are all grouped together) there is no joking

relationship whatever, but between you and your father's parents there is a regular joking relationship all right, and it is very common. This is also extended to the grandparents of the father, but not those of the mother.

Well, this seems to be all for the present. Naturally I would like to know your reaction to the above data in comparison with the Jicarilla, Lipan, Kiowa Apache, Mescalero, and Chiricahua. If you have time, drop me a line about it sometime. My address will be Hassayampa Mt. Club, Prescott, Ariz., for the rest of the summer. Am planning to work over among the Tonto this summer if possible, but this will be my address.

It is important to note that the answers to questions 2, 3, 4, and 5 are based mainly on White Mt. work, and so do not stand definitely for Cibecue, San Carlos, Southern Tonto, and Northern Tonto usage. I have not worked out the usages for these last four groups completely yet, and there may arise differences, though I don't think they will be important ones, as the whole scheme of the kinship system among all five of the W. Apache groups is about the same. If any important differences do exist in the above usages, they have not yet shown themselves in the work thus far with the other four groups.

I hope that all goes well with your work, and when you get time, drop me a line and please give me the same data for the Apache that you have worked with as I have given you for the Western Apache in this letter. It might prove a great help to me in locating customs here.

Sincerely,
GRENVILLE GOODWIN

July 28, 1935
17 Broadmoor Ave.
Colo. Spgs., Colo.

Dear Morrie,

I must apologize for keeping your Jicarilla paper so long, almost two weeks now.[48] The truth is that I did not get it till the 24th, when it was sent on to me at Payson, Ariz., from Prescott, just the day I was leaving for Colorado. Hence the delay.

Read your paper with a great deal of interest. It certainly covers all the main points and leaves one with an excellent picture of the culture. Thanks a lot for sending it on. There are quite a few leads in it that am sure will be of great help to me.

About the grandparent bugaboo you speak of among the Jicarilla: the special punishments only administered by grandparents, I have not yet found among the W. Apache, though in further work they may possibly turn up. The grandparents, particularly on the maternal side, take a share in the disciplining of children all right, and quite often this is more noticeable than that administered by parents when it is in verbal form, as some of them are more prone to shout threats at disobedient and annoying grandchildren than are parents. But that is as far as it seems to go. Later on, if more should turn up on this point, will let you know.

Was interested to hear of your contemplated paper comparing S. Athapascan kinship traits. When are you going to get it out?[49]

For the past week have been working among the Southern Tonto group at Payson, Ariz., with Gifford, one of Kroeber's men from Berkeley. He is the one who wrote the Yavapai paper. He has been sent on a six months' tour of the Southwest, to fill out a culture element list with plusses or minuses for existing or lacking traits among all Southwest peoples. It is seemingly a purely statistical approach (I don't

---

[48] This was the manuscript of a paper summarizing the main features of Jicarilla culture that was eventually published as Opler 1936c.
[49] This projected paper was published as Opler 1936b.

74

know how satisfactory), with the purpose of filling in the gaps now existent in published material on the Southwest. Whether or not monographic work is being done in the field now does not seem to matter, as Gifford intends to work all peoples. I just mention all this because he speaks of going to Jicarilla and Mescalero to work the Apache there, and so I thought you might be interested. I worked with him a week because he and Kroeber asked me to. The method is all right as far as it goes, but it doesn't go very deep, as you can understand when you know that it only takes six days to run through the complete culture element list from A to Z. It seems purely statistical and a way of getting existing traits over a wide area in a hurry. I mentioned your wide experience among the Apache in New Mexico to him, and so he will probably look you up.[50] Any data that you have given me on the Apache with whom you have worked, of course, I have not passed on to him, so he knows nothing more about the peoples than what is already published, and about the three bands of the Chiricahua, and about the Lipan living with the Mescalero at Mescalero. Will be interested to see what you think of Gifford.

Am just up here for a few days in Colorado, and expect to return to Arizona on Thursday next, to Prescott, where my address will be for the rest of the summer. Hope to get in some Northern Tonto work later on.

Sincerely,
G. Goodwin

P.S. I hope you land your job.[51]

---

[50] The person referred to was Edward W. Gifford. He never got in touch with me.

[51] At this point the funds I had accumulated for sustained field work had been exhausted, and I had been invited by Scudder Mekeel to apply for the position of anthropologist in a unit of the Bureau of Indian Affairs which he had been chosen to head. I obtained the position and held it until the serious illness of my wife dictated that I give up the wandering life it demanded. Since many of my assignments were on Apache Indian reservations, this position prolonged my opportunity to remain in contact with the Apache and gather field data from them.

Aug. 12, 1936
17 Broadmoor Ave.
Colorado Springs, Colorado

Dear Morrie,

Sorry not to have written you before, but I have been very busy since arriving here and have not had time. Better late than never, though. I guess by now you are at White River, and trust that things are going well and that you are able to accomplish something in the way of organizing these people.[52]

I enclose a rough drawing such as you requested. As you will see, the whole of the San Carlos Res. is not shown on it, nor the whole extent of the bands and groups whose territory originally extended over it. But you will be able to get a rough idea from it of the location at present of the various groups and bands on the San Carlos Res.

1. The people living east of the main store at Bylas. They are mostly composed of people of the San Carlos group, with a few Southern Tonto among them. There are also a few White Mt. people among them.

2. The people living west of the main store at Bylas, composed of E. and W. White Mt. people.

3. The Calva settlement, a newly made farming site. The people here are about one-third from the San Carlos group, the remainder being White Mt. people (mostly Western White Mt.).

4. The farms beginning at the old highway bridge ("six mile bridge") and extending up river on the San Carlos Riv. till a gap of no farming occurs, below Peridot. These people are mostly from the San Carlos group.

5. The Peridot area. These people are mostly of the San Carlos group.

---

[52] When I was sent to Arizona to help implement the Indian Reorganization Act among the Western Apache, I asked Goodwin to supply me with certain information about the modern groupings of the Western Apache and their relations to the older social units. This letter was his response. As his remarks at the end of the letter indicate, just before I entered upon my Indian Service duties, I had had another meeting with Goodwin at Ruidoso, New Mexico, near the Mescalero Reservation.

6. These people, all the farms extending up the San Carlos River and Seven Mile Wash, from Tiffany's store up, are mostly San Carlos, with a few Southern Tonto and a very few Northern Tonto.

7. These people are mostly San Carlos, with some Southern Tonto and a very few Northern Tonto. This is a newly constructed farming site.

8. This is the new settlement plan for the Tonto supposedly, now in progress.

As you can see from the map, both bands of the White Mt. group still have incorporated within the present limits of the San Carlos Res. a large piece of their original territory. But with the San Carlos group this is not the case. All the farming sites of these latter people are now located within the original territory of one of their four original bands (the San Carlos band), there being none of the farming sites in their old band territories left to them now, within the reservation. As for the Tonto, they are entirely on San Carlos group territory now, there being none of their old territory incorporated within either the San Carlos or Ft. Apache reservations.

I hope that this is the data which you desired. Am leaving for the East today, but in case you want to reach me, you can do so through this address, and your letter will be forwarded.

I enjoyed our visit at Ruidoso a great deal. I would have liked to stay longer, but it is better to wait a little and then we can go through the whole problem of the Apache from the beginning. From what you said about the Apache you have worked with, I could see that just about all the existing gaps on the Apache as a whole can be filled in with the data which I now have on the Western Apache, so that a very complete picture of the Southern Athapascans will be possible shortly.

Give my regards to Mrs. Opler, and best of luck to you.

Sincerely,
GRENVILLE GOODWIN

Feb. 6, 1937
133 North Main St.
Tucson, Ariz.

Dear Morrie,

Thanks for your letter of Jan. 14. Oklahoma City does not seem such a great distance away, and I am glad that you plan to be back in the Southwest next summer.

The paper on the Apache clans which you refer to was published in the *New Mexico Historical Review,* Vol. VIII, No. 3. It really is not what it ought to be, and in writing it again I would make some changes in the contents, due to more recent work.

I have not yet received a copy of your ethnobotany bulletin from New Mex. University, but maybe it will come soon.[53] I did receive your reprint of the paper on Southwestern Athapascan kinship systems, though, and I don't think I have thanked you for it. In your data on the Western Apache there are some points I would like to ask you about, as they seem to be at variance with data that I have. The best thing to do is list them below.[54]

1. In the chart of the Western Apache kinship system, you give the sibling terms K and L as used between ego and his mother's brother's children, and between ego and his father's sister's children. I believe that I once gave you information to this effect, at least for ego and his father's sister's children, but that was based on erroneous work done in the field in 1932. I have since not been able to find this usage, and in the kinship chart and list of terms that I sent you last spring I am sure that I did not give it as a term usage. During the time that you spent among the Western Apache last summer did you find this correct or incorrect?

---

[53] See Opler 1936a.
[54] During this period Goodwin was constantly correcting and amplifying his materials on kinship and social organization. He was very good about letting me know of new discoveries, refinements, and the correction of past errors; but inevitably, since we were both very busy and usually on the move, there were time lags and oversights. These were responsible for the minor errors in the very compressed comparative paper to which Goodwin alludes.

2. The kinship terms which you list for the Western Apache (White Mt. group) — are they recordings of terms as I supplied them to you, or are they here given as recorded by some other person? The reason I ask is that most of them differ from the recordings of the same terms that I sent you last spring (some only in minor detail). If you found my recording of these terms erroneous in the light of work done by someone else, I would very much like to know it. Possibly the terms you give are recorded by yourself, or Harry Hoijer, or Dave Mandelbaum. Except for the slight differences in the recording of them, they are the same as the ones which I have obtained.[55]

3. In the footnote on page 628 you say that "Western Apache kinship shows but little variation throughout its range." This is true enough of White Mountain, Cibecue, San Carlos, and Southern Tonto, where we find only one term which is new from White Mt. to the last three groups, which use a third sibling term denoting age difference from ego added to the two that you list for the White Mt. But among the Northern Tonto there are at least three terms commonly used in place of those for corresponding positions by the rest of the Western Apache, which are entirely different. I'm not quite sure that it is possible to say that there is but slight variation throughout the Western Apache kinship systems for this reason, at least insofar as the difference of the terms goes.

4. On page 629, paragraph three, you say that joking relationships are a clan matter, directed towards the members of the father's clan. I would be more inclined to interpret it the other way around — *that joking is extended to the father's clan by ego and they to him because all members of the father's clan are considered potential cross-cousins to ego.* From your own experience among the White Mt. and Cibecue Apache last summer, would you not say the same as I now? However, if you still hold to the interpretation given in your paper, I would very much like to know. There is also a joking relation between ego and one grandparent which may exist

---

[55] The Western Apache terms I used had been recorded by Harry Hoijer, the specialist on the Apachean languages.

and is recognized, though not universally practiced. This grandparent is the father's mother (White Mt. usage). I believe you did not mention this in your paper.

Well, you see I stuck to the good old number four. On the whole I think the paper is swell, and I can't tell you how much I enjoyed it. Something like it was certainly a very necessary and helpful contribution to Southern Athapascan data. I hope you will not take these points the wrong way. It is done with the best of intentions and merely for the purpose of setting right any false impression concerning the Western Apache which I may have given you. I wish you would write and tell me which, if any, of the four points I bring up here you would make changes in after your firsthand contact with some of thc Western Apache. I may have a paper published before very long, and it offers a chance to correct any errors which may now be included in your paper, due to me or a misunderstanding on your part.

I hope that all goes well with you and Mrs. Opler. Best of luck in your work, and write me when you have time.

Sincerely,
G. GOODWIN

Feb. 10, 1937
133 North Main St.
Tucson, Ariz.

Dear Morrie,

Thanks for your prompt reply. Yes, I remember now about your asking if there were any changes to be made in ego's generation, and so the slip-up about the use of sibling terms for cross-cousins in the White Mountain group is my fault. It does not matter so much anyway, as you say. In this article that I have coming out in the *Anthropologist* before long (on clans),[56] I slipped in a footnote concerning the above, and you will find a copy of it at the foot of the enclosed paper. Am not sure that it will be included with the article, but it may.

I am sorry that I failed to explain to you the cross-cousin joking relationship. I thought that I had, but apparently I did not make it clear. On the enclosed page is the section from my paper dealing with this matter and also with some other joking relationships. I think this will answer part of your questions. Cross-cousin terms, though often applied to men of other generations than ego, unrelated by blood, are first of all *for cross-cousins by blood*. Secondly, they are applied to *persons of the same generation as ego in the father's clan or phratry* and to *children of male members of ego's clan or phratry who are of the same generation as ego* (*children* are of same generation as ego). The persons involved in this second usage are considered cross-cousins, though actually they may not be so related by blood. This second usage is where the majority of the joking relationships occur, and this will answer your question concerning joking being extended to cross-cousins on the maternal side, for the fathers of the children mentioned above are very often extended clan siblings of ego's mother. When I said in my letter to you "joking is extended to the father's clan by ego and they to him because all members of the father's clan are considered potential cross-cousins to ego," I meant that cross-cousin terms can be extended to almost any member of

---

[56] See Goodwin 1937.

the father's clan, regardless of generation, as well as the joking relationship (when not closely related by blood), and thus they are all capable of being treated as cross-cousins and joked.

The nature of the cross-cousin joking relationship between members of the same sex is as follows: wrestling in fun, general roughhousing (the only joking relationship where this occurs and which marks it off in the Western Apache mind as the joking relationship par excellence), playing pranks such as hiding each other's horses even to the extent of causing several days' search for the animals, filling clothes with cockleburs, etc., making up wild tales about each other and circulating them, general good-natured banter, threats to steal each other's mates (though this would never be done), and other pranks. When of opposite sex, the individuals cannot touch each other but can indulge in all sorts of joking, the most common form being to offer oneself in marriage or threaten to run off with the other person, or to chide in fun about each other's love life, as well as general banter along other lines and small pranks. But even with this joking relationship, young people are admonished by their elders not to go too far, that it might end in a serious fight; and this has apparently happened several times.

I could find no fear of witchcraft and mishap between cross-cousins or real avoidance relationships, as I believe you found at Jicarilla. But in joking with the mate of your cross-cousin of the same sex, you usually do so in the cross-cousin's presence. This seems rather like your Jicarilla data, doesn't it? But the joking seems to stop short by some distance from that in like cases among the Jicarilla.

I believe that I forgot to tell you that both the father's parents and ego may observe a joking relationship in mild vein, but there is no recognized joking relationship with maternal grandparents.

This seems to answer all your questions, and I hope that it gives a clear picture. If you still do not understand it, let me know and I think that it will be possible to clarify any points that may arise.

Sincerely,
G. GOODWIN

Dear Morrie,

I have read your paper on the relation of kinship terminology to social classification with a great deal of interest.[57]
Am sorry to have kept it so long, but when it arrived I was
in the process of finishing up a manuscript which had to be
sent off as soon as possible. I hope that the delay in returning
your paper has not inconvenienced you.

The Western Apache data which you use in the paper
in no way conflicts with any of my material, and I feel it is
sound and a good example of what you are trying to prove.
You certainly have a good argument by the use of the Apache
data, unless the Apache prove to be an exception to the norm
or are in any way in the process of dissolving or readjusting
the practices which Radcliffe-Brown might call inconsistencies.
It seems to me, though, that your point would be even
stronger if you had compared the so-called "consistencies"
and "inconsistencies" in toto and shown just how they lined
up in numbers.

Another point upon which I wish you could have
enlarged, merely from the data from Apache peoples, is that
on page 12. You say here that it may be because two or more
terminological choices are implicit in the totality of behavior
patterns which surround any one relative, that different or
the same terms are used in one Apache tribe or another for
the same relative. A list of what these terminological choices
are among the Apache and any rules which might limit them,
such as the sex of the individuals concerned or the kind of
blood relatives they are, might be helpful. However, any such
rules which may exist may be apparent enough in your discussion of the different tribes. On pages 13 and 14 you list

---

[57] I had sent Goodwin the manuscript that was later to appear as
Opler 1937. In this paper my intention was to show the limitations of
employing kinship terminology as the sole guide to appropriate behavior
toward kin. I sought to demonstrate that for various reasons persons
to whom identical kin terms were addressed were nevertheless treated
differently. Since I included examples from Western Apache material
furnished by Goodwin, I wanted him to see the paper in advance of
publication.

some of the other things besides kinship terminology which perpetuate certain behavior patterns. There are two very important factors which control behavorism between certain kin and affinal relatives also, which I have come across in my work. One of these is the personal contact between the individuals concerned at the time, and the other is the degree of blood relationship which may exist. You apparently take into consideration the first of these in your discussion of the Jicarilla child and his maternal grandparent, but among Western Apache it may control the behavior towards other relatives, also. I don't know if the degree of blood relationship between individuals has much, if any, control over behavior in the Apache peoples you have studied, but if it does, I think it is a point which should be mentioned. Among the White Mt. Apache it influences the difference in behavior patterns toward individuals who are addressed by identical kin terms.

These are all the comments which come to mind. I only hope they will prove of some use and wish that they might be more constructive. They are merely additions and, as you see, do not in any way disagree with your statements. Thanks for giving me the opportunity to read over your paper, and I hope that it will appear soon in the *Anthropologist*. It should prove an important contribution.

Sincerely,
G. GOODWIN

Dear Morrie,

Thanks for your information on the painted buffalo hide.[58] Concerning the history of the object I know nothing and do not believe there are any data to be had along these lines. It is in the Taylor collection at Colorado Springs. The reason that I thought it might be Mescalero in origin is that there are figures on it which to me seem unmistakably representations of *gá•n*. However, I do not know how the Jicarilla masked dancers are pictorially represented, if at all, and, as you say, it may be Jicarilla. I wish you could see it sometime.

I only saw a small portion of Gifford's trait lists, but he had several things which were at variance with my material, and it would not be surprising if you had found the same true. I worked with him in the field for about a week once. He most certainly is well acquainted with material culture objects and the mechanical side of a culture, but because of his laboring under a severe physical handicap (deafness), he does make unintentional errors at times. His technique in the gathering of material for these lists (one which the character of lists enforces, as you can well see) makes the data very spotty, with overemphasis on some points which tends to be misleading. About the "Huachuca Apache," I was puzzled also. He must either refer to one of the three Chiricahua bands, presumably what you call the Chiricahua proper, ·or those Apache scouts and their families who are stationed at Ft. Huachuca, Arizona, and who are composed of San Carlos and White Mountain people. As I understand it, the Huachuca Mts. in Ariz., were in the western portion of the territory claimed by the Chiricahua proper.[59]

---

[58] A picture of a painted buffalo hide, with Apache-like masked dancer figures on it, had been sent to me for tribal identification.

[59] Because of Goodwin's presence and assistance, the margin of error in the Western Apache trait lists recorded by Gifford was fairly low. His surveys of the other Apache tribes are so faulty, however, that they are worse than useless. For one thing, he does not use comparable

My work is progressing very well, and I am well started on writing up the first section of it, social organization. The two papers which Harry and Mrs. Parsons mentioned were one on the character and function of the clan in a Southern Athapascan group (White Mt.) and the other on the religion of the White Mt. Apache, which includes a discussion of shamans, rituals, holy power, cosmology, etc. I would like you to see them very much, as I mentioned them some time ago to you in a letter. Unfortunately I have no copy of the first now, but it is scheduled to come out in the July *Anthropologist,* and I will send you a reprint of it. I should have a copy of the second paper available in a few days, and if I can get hold of it, will send it on to you.

Sincerely,
G. Goodwin

---

social units in his analysis; he compares bands with tribes and even invents units that never existed, such as the Huachuca Apache. The results of his investigation of the Apache, against which I warn, are to be found in Gifford 1940.

July 25, 1938
401 Delgado St.
Santa Fe, New Mexico

Dear Morrie,

By this time you have probably left Reed College and gone east, but this letter, I hope, will be forwarded to you.[60] First of all, I want to thank you for the copy of the Jicarilla myths. I like the way it is gotten out and the method you have used in indexing the cultural material contained within the myths. The myths in themselves form a valuable collection, and I had not realized the Jicarilla mythology would be so voluminous.[61]

Secondly, I have a few questions to ask you. Recently I have been trying to get together a pair of dolls, one man, one woman, from each of the Apache divisions: Western Apache, Chiricahua, Mescalero, Lipan, Kiowa Apache, and Jicarilla. The costumes of these dolls are to be made as accurately as possible, and the whole collection, I hope, is to be used as an exhibition showing the differences and similarities in costume. I am also doing the same for model baby carriers for each of the six Apache divisions. We now have the dolls and baby carriers from Western Apache, Jicarilla, and Lipan, and a pair of Mescalero dolls have been ordered. A recent trip to Mescalero to take in the Fourth of July celebration gave an opportunity to contact a Lipan woman and a Mescalero woman to make the dolls for me. It is about the Lipan dolls and baby carrier, which have already been made and sent to me, that I wish to ask you. I had somewhat expected the Lipan costume to be different from that which these dolls indicate, if they are correctly made.

---

[60] I had taught at Reed College, Portland, Oregon, for an academic year but had accepted a post at Claremont Colleges, Claremont, California, for the following year. During the summer my wife and I went east to visit relatives and to collect personal effects.

[61] I had sent Goodwin a copy of my *Myths and Tales of the Jicarilla Apache Indians* (Opler 1938). Goodwin's collection of Western Apache myths and tales was published the next year in the same series (Goodwin 1939).

1. The man is dressed in a buckskin shirt of the Plains type, but lacking the front and rear triangular flaps which ordinarily hang down from the neck, as in this sketch. [See fig. 4a.] His buckskin breeches are the regular Plains type also. His moccasins do not differ essentially from the Mescalero type of men's moccasins with a line of fringe running down the top from instep to toe. His hair is braided also in the regular Plains way. His costume is what I had expected, except for the absence of the triangular piece on the shirt. Does this description tally with what you have on the Lipan man's costume? If not, in what respects is it different?

2. The woman's costume in all details seems to be almost identical with that of the Mescalero women, and even Chiricahua and Western Apache women. The woman is dressed in a wide poncho type of shirt, which is well fringed and hangs down over her shoulders and arms to just below her waist. The skirt is of the regular type, fringed and hanging to just below the knees. On each side it has two small, fringed, tab-like pendants. [See fig. 4b.] The mocassins do not seem to differ from those of Mescalero women: the high type folded back over a time or two. [See fig. 4c.] The only thing which was new to me was the method of doing the hair. The woman had her hair done in a sort of a club at the back of the head. It was wrapped with buckskin and looked something like the drawing below. [See fig. 4d.] The drawing isn't so good, but it will show you what I mean.

Is this the costume of the Lipan woman as you understand it? If not, in what details does it differ?

3. The baby carrier type is identical with those I have seen from the Mescalero and Chiricahua, with one exception. This is a sort of footboard under and along the side where the baby's feet come. [See fig. 4e.] When the baby is in the carrier, the soles of his feet would rest against this footboard. The little side pieces of wood apparently hold it in place.

Is this the Lipan type of baby carrier as you have had it described to you? This one also has the buckskin flaps on the sides for lacing the baby in, but I have not shown them in the drawing.

The Lipan woman who made these things was Augustina Zwazwa. You probably know her. She could not be over

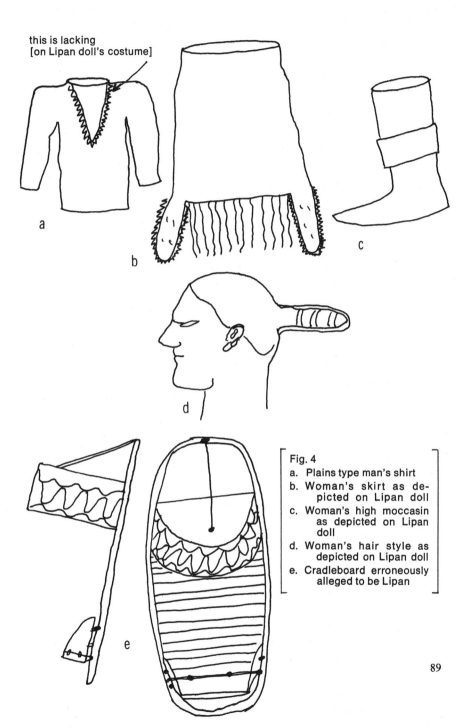

this is lacking
[on Lipan doll's costume]

a

b

c

d

e

Fig. 4
a. Plains type man's shirt
b. Woman's skirt as depicted on Lipan doll
c. Woman's high moccasin as depicted on Lipan doll
d. Woman's hair style as depicted on Lipan doll
e. Cradleboard erroneously alleged to be Lipan

89

forty-five at most and so, of course, would have no firsthand knowledge of old costumes. As a matter of fact, she said she did not know about these things but was going to ask an old Lipan woman, a relative of hers, and make the things according to her instructions. Now I wonder if she has not confused some Mescalero elements with true Lipan ones in the making of the dolls and the baby carrier. Such a thing would be possible, living as she does among the Mescalero. It may be that the details are perfectly correct and that the Lipan costume and dress were not essentially different from the Mescalero. What is your feeling about this? I would appreciate any information which you could give.

I was down at the Gila Pueblo in Globe not long ago. Ted Sayles, who sent you the chart of Apache archaeological artifacts in hopes that you could fill in the blanks for the Chiricahua, said that he had not heard from you at all. When you have time, could you please let him know how you are progressing with it or when you think you will have time to get at it? I know you probably have had all the work you could handle, but if you could just drop him a line about it, I would appreciate it.[62]

Things go on as usual in Santa Fe. People arrive and leave, and we are sorry that we shall not see you and Catherine among them. We enjoyed the Mescalero celebration immensely. I have wanted to see it for a long time. The similarities and differences were very interesting.

Hoping that all goes well with Catherine and you and that you both have a good summer.

Sincerely,

G. GOODWIN

---

[62] Because of the disruptions due to moving, I was far behind in my correspondence, but shortly after this I tried to supply Dr. Sayles with the information for which he had asked.

Oct. 22, 1938
401 Delgado St.
Santa Fe, New Mexico

Dear Morrie,

I received your card last August concerning my questions on Lipan costume. Though my brother took some photos at the Mescalero Fourth of July celebration, they were unsatisfactory, as he had some sort of newfangled film which he got in the camera upside down, or something to that effect.

Since writing to you last time, I have acquired a very good pair of Mescalero dolls, one man and one woman, showing the old type costume. In almost every detail this is identical with that shown by the Lipan dolls I wrote you about last summer. Even the hair style of the woman is the same, with the hair done up in a club at the back of the head. The woman's dress is a fringed buckskin shirt and a poncho-like upper garment, also fringed. The moccasins are of the tall, boot-like variety. Have you had a chance to examine your Lipan and Mescalero notes and see how the descriptions compare with them? Another point was the Lipan cradle, which, except for a wooden footboard, is the same as the Chiricahua and Mescalero. As we are getting ready to prepare the museum exhibit in Tucson, in which these dolls will appear, I would greatly appreciate any information you can give me on these points as soon as possible.[63]

Another point I wished to ask you about: You remember the summer before this last one, when you were here, you showed me a set of drawings and watercolors of Jicarilla sand paintings, done by a Jicarilla crippled boy. As I recall it, you had a duplicate set which the boy had sent you to sell for him. The House of Navajo Religion, which amounts to an exhibi-

---

[63] In a letter of October 25, 1938 (one of two letters to Goodwin of which I have a copy), I answered his inquiries about Apache tribal characteristics in respect to dress, hair style, and the cradle board. Among other things, I pointed out that the Lipan used a rawhide carrier, rather than a cradle with frame, canopy, and foot piece, for transporting the baby, and that the Lipan woman's hair, dressed in the style represented by his doll (there were other styles according to age), followed the conformation of the back of the head rather than extending stiffly behind like a club.

tion hall of Navajo sand paintings, here in Santa Fe, has collected hundreds of Navajo sand paintings and now has them on file. They are rather interested in obtaining some Apache sand paintings to add to their files. Do you think it would be possible to obtain a set of those such as you had from the Jicarilla? Would this boy be willing to paint them a set, and if so, how can I get in touch with him? First of all, I want to make it clear that the paintings would merely be filed and possibly exhibited in the museum sometime. There would be no publication of them of any sort. Secondly, I fully realize that you probably went to a great deal of trouble in getting drawings of these paintings and that quite reasonably you may wish to keep them to yourself till after you publish on them. If this is the case, I fully sympathize with you and would not think of intruding in any way on your Jicarilla scoop. However, please let me know your stand on this.[64]

I went up to the Jicarilla festival this September for the first time and enjoyed it immensely. It certainly was vastly different from any Apache ceremony I had ever seen and, at least in outward appearance, strikingly like the Picurís race we saw.[65]

We have had a pleasant summer here, and now that autumn has come, things are quiet again. Let me know how your new job is going. It sounds like a good one.

Sincerely,

G. GOODWIN

---

[64] The "crippled boy" was a Jicarilla man who knew the details of the Holiness Rite (sometimes misnamed the Jicarilla Bear Dance) because he had been a patient in it a number of times in an attempt to cure an advanced case of arthritis. He had not given me a set of sand painting drawings for sale but had, at my request, prepared a set for an Indian Service official who had seen the one he had made for me. I acted as a go-between in a like manner for the House of Navajo Religion, now known as the Museum of Navajo Ceremonial Art. In response to Goodwin's concern about interfering with my "scoop," I wrote: "I would not want to put any restrictions on the use of the paintings, except that I think it is proper to ask that they not be published until after I have published." For the details of the Holiness Rite, see Opler 1943.

[65] The festival which Goodwin saw was the Jicarilla Apache Ceremonial Relay Race. Since it was inspired in part by a similar race at Picurís, Goodwin's reaction is a natural one. See Opler 1944.

Nov. 13, 1938
P.O. Gen. Delivery
Tucson, Ariz.

Dear Morrie,

Thanks for your letter concerning the Lipan and Jicarilla information. I had rather suspected that the cradle was an adaptation of the Mescalero-Chiricahua form. Thanks also for the photo of the Lipan shirt. I gather that I am to keep it, but if this isn't so, just let me know, and I'll send it back to you.

Was very glad to know that you would try for the Jicarilla sand paintings. I most certainly appreciate your willingness. The House of Navajo Religion will, of course, be glad to pay the $15 and any additional costs of materials and postage. They also guarantee not to publish reproductions of them till after you have published, and for that matter they have no plans or wishes to publish them. They merely want them to put on file. When you have found out from the Jicarilla if you can get the pictures made, will you please write directly to the House of Navajo Religion in Santa Fe, P.O. Box 445. They will send you the money as soon as you want it.

I don't know if you have the facts about the House of Navajo Religion or not. It was founded by a Miss Wheelwright, a well-to-do woman from Mass., who has lived in New Mexico for some years and who has taken a great interest in the Navajo, particularly in recording their ceremonies. Harry Hoijer did some linguistic work for her once, which you probably have heard of. About a year or two ago she put up a building not far from the Laboratory of Anthropology, to house her collection of sand paintings, etc. She has incorporated this into the establishment called the House of Navajo Religion, which has as its aim the furthering of recording of Navajo religious material and of filing away same in order that research students may utilize it. Though the project started as more or less of a hobby with Miss Wheelwright, I think it has chances of really developing into something constructive and useful. My interest in it is because I was elected a trustee not long ago.

On the way down to Tucson I stopped in at Mescalero and saw Sam Kenoi. I also met Duncan Belacho and Dan Nicholas at his camp.[66] Was very glad to meet the latter as I had heard so much about him from you. He wanted to know about you and said he would write but was too lazy to do so. He wanted your address, which I gave him. Both he and Sam were delighted that you were no longer in the Indian Service, as they said you were much too good a man for that![67] Dan said to tell you that everything was fine with him, that though he had had some trouble a while back, everything was straightened out now. He said you would know what he meant. Thanks again for your much appreciated cooperation on the Jicarilla paintings.

Sincerely,

G. GOODWIN

---

[66] These were Chiricahua friends and informants to whom I had introduced Goodwin.

[67] At this time I was teaching at Claremont Colleges, Claremont, California. None of these men had any great liking for the Indian Service. Sam Kenoi, in particular, had a long history of feuding with the agency officials. Consequently, this was probably as great a compliment as these Indians could pay to their anthropologist friend.

Oct. 1, 1939
Apt. 3 S
1310 E. Hyde Park Blvd.
Chicago, Ill.

Dear Morrie,

Well, here we are in Chicago, and I'll give you three guesses as to why we are here. Perhaps you already know, but anyway we are here for the winter while I take on some education. It's something we have been wanting to do for the last two years now, and we finally got here for better or for worse. It should do me a lot of good, and the courses look very interesting.

Thanks a lot for the reprint of the Tonkawa article.[68] I read it through with interest. I am sorry that we could not stop in and see you on the way from Carmel to Tucson. We both would have liked to, but we were in a great hurry to get to Arizona, and the day we passed your home territory it was raining and cold and about all we could think of was getting over the mountains to the dry desert. I hope you will excuse us. However, you can be sure that the next time we should come by we will descend on you. It would be good to get together again. As a matter of fact, we won't be such distant neighbors as we now are. I have an appointment at the University of Arizona as research associate in the Department of Anthropology, and as soon as we are finished here (I hope within a year), we are going back to Tucson to settle permanently. Maybe you and Catherine will be going through Tucson sometime and could stop with us.[69]

Hope that all goes well with you and your work and Catherine. Jan sends her best to you both.

Sincerely,
G. Goodwin

---

[68] See Opler 1939.

[69] These pleasant prospects were not to materialize. Not long after this letter was written, Goodwin was stricken with a malignant brain tumor and died in June, 1940.

Bibliographic References

Abel, Annie Heloise (ed.)

1915   *The Official Correspondence of James S. Calhoun While Indian Agent at Santa Fe and Superintendent of Indian Affairs in New Mexico.* Washington, D.C.: U.S. Government Printing Office.

Basso, Keith H.

1970   *The Cibecue Apache.* New York: Holt, Rinehart and Winston.

Gifford, E. W.

1940   *Culture Element Distributions: XII. Apache-Pueblo. Anthropological Records,* vol. 4, no. 1. Berkeley: University of California Press.

Goodwin, Grenville

1933   Clans of the Western Apache. *New Mexico Historical Review* 8: 176–182.

1935   The Social Divisions and Economic Life of the Western Apache. *American Anthropologist* 37: 55–64.

1937   The Characteristics and Function of Clan in a Southern Athapascan Culture. *American Anthropologist* 39: 394–407.

1939   *Myths and Tales of the White Mountain Apache.* Memoirs of the American Folklore Society, vol. 33. New York: Published for the American Folklore Society by J. J. Augustin.

1942   *The Social Organization of the Western Apache.* Chicago: University of Chicago Press.

1971   *Western Apache Raiding and Warfare: From the Notes of Grenville Goodwin* (ed. by Keith H. Basso). Tucson: University of Arizona Press.

Opler, Morris E.

1936a (with Edward F. Castetter). *The Ethnobiology of the Chiricahua and Mescalero Apache. A. The Use of Plants for Foods, Beverages and Narcotics* (Ethnobiological Studies in the American Southwest, 3). *University of New Mexico Bulletin,* whole no. 297; Biological Series, vol. 4, no. 5. Albuquerque: University of New Mexico Press.

1936b The Kinship Systems of the Southern Athabaskan-Speaking Tribes. *American Anthropologist* 38: 620–633.

1936c A Summary of Jicarilla Apache Culture. *American Anthropologist* 38: 202–223.

1937   Apache Data Concerning the Relation of Kinship Terminology to Social Classification. *American Anthropologist* 39: 201–212.

1938   *Myths and Tales of the Jicarilla Apache Indians.* Memoirs of the American Folklore Society, vol. 31. New York: G. E. Stechert Co.

1939   A Description of a Tonkawa Peyote Meeting Held in 1902. *American Anthropologist* 41: 433–439.

1943   *The Character and Derivation of the Jicarilla Holiness Rite. University of New Mexico Bulletin,* whole no. 390; Anthropological Series, vol. 4, no. 3. Albuquerque: University of New Mexico Press.

1944   The Jicarilla Apache Ceremonial Relay Race. *American Anthropologist* 46: 75–97.

1972   Cause and Effect in Apachean Agriculture, Division of Labor, Residence Patterns, and Girls' Puberty Rites. *American Anthropologist* 74: 1133–1146.

Reichard, Gladys A.

1928   *Social Life of the Navajo Indians, with Some Attention to Minor Ceremonies.* Columbia University Contributions to Anthropology, vol. 7. New York: Columbia University Press.

Acknowledgments

THIS BOOK is part of a comparative Apachean project for which the author received generous support from the National Endowment for the Humanities through a Senior Fellowship and from the University of Oklahoma Faculty Research Committee.

The interest and skills of Elaine Nantkes of the University of Arizona Press have greatly facilitated the process of seeing the book through publication. For assistance at every stage in the preparation of the manuscript, I am indebted to my wife, Lucille R. Opler.

M. E. O.

Index

Affinal terms, 41, 42
Agave, 34 *n*. *See also* Mescal
Agriculture, 68; crops, 44; degree of
    dependence on, 52, 53; division of
    labor, 44; dry farming, 45; irriga-
    tion, 44, 45; practices, 35 *n*, 42–
    45; practices reflected in myth-
    ology, 44; techniques, 44–45; use
    of digging stick, 44. *See also* Corn
    plants; Snake; Turkey
Apache Mansos, 35 *n*, 42
Apachean-speaking tribes, 67 *n*
Arivaipa Apache, 20. *See also* San
    Carlos Apache
Avoidance, 42

Ball game, 27
Baskets, use of in trade, 52
Basso, Keith, 11
Belacho, Duncan, 94
Benedict, Ruth, 12
Blackened One, Mescalero Apache
    masked dancer, 63 *n*
Blumensohn, Jules, 19, 63, 63 *n*.
    See also Henry, Jules
Buffalo, range of, 31
Bureau of Indian Affairs, 75 *n*
Bylas, Arizona, 27, 76

Calhoun, James S., 33
Calva, Arizona, 27, 76
Canyon Day, Arizona, 25–26
Cave storage, 45
Cedar Creek, 25

Chieftainship, 26
Chiricahua Apache, 8, 25, 31, 50, 63;
    bands, 30; kinship terms, 19, 24;
    southern band, 28 *n*. *See also*
    Warm Springs Apache
Chiricahua Mountains, 29
Cibecue Apache, 20
Clan, 38, 40, 68, 78; designs, 40,
    41; leadership, 40; migration
    myths, 36; organization, 19 *n*. *See
    also* Coyotero Apache; White
    Mountain Apache
Columbia University, 24, 24 *n*
Corn plants, 43
Corn pollen, 43
Cornmeal, 43
Coyotero Apache, 20, 30, 31; clans,
    26. *See also* White Mountain
    Apache
Cummings, Dean Byron, 23 *n*

Dewey Flats, 27
Dos Cabezas Mountain, 29
Douglas, Arizona, 29
Dragoon Mountains, 28, 29

East Fork of White River, 26, 27
Economic life, 51
Edwards, Silas John, 42, 63 *n*

Field Museum of Natural History,
    19
Flute, 28

101

Fort Apache, 26, 27
Fort Bowie, 29
Fort McDowell Apache, 32
Four, as a ritual number, 58

Gifford, Edward W., 74, 75 *n*, 85
Gila Pueblo, 90
Gila River, 26
Gillin, John P., 12
Girl's puberty rite, 22, 43; use of
  drinking tube and scratcher in, 27
Goodwin, Grenville, 7, 8, 9, 11, 12,
  13, 14, 15
Graham Mountain, 21
Ground caches, 45

Headwoman, 36
Henry, Jules, 12, 19 *n. See also*
  Blumensohn, Jules
Herzfeld, Regina Flannery, 12
Heye Museum, 19 *n*
Hoijer, Harry, 12, 24 *n*, 65, 70, 79
Hoop and pole game, 27
Hopi Indians, 52
House of Navajo Religion, 91–92, 93
House types, 58–59, 63
Huachuca Apache, a misnomer, 85
Huachuca Mountains, 85

Individualism, in ceremonial life,
  52–53
Inheritance, of land, 43

Janos, Chihuahua, Mexico, 29
Jicarilla Apache, 8, 50, 93;
  ceremonial relay race, 92, 92 *n;*
  grandparent bugaboo, 72; Holiness
  Rite, 92 *n;* masked dancers, 85;
  mythology, 87; sand paintings,
  91–92, 93; social organization, 65
Kenoi, Sam, 42 *n*, 94
Kinship, importance of, 38 *n;* self-
  reciprocal terms, 70; sibling terms,
  28; terms and behavior, 70–73;
  usages, 78, 81–82
Kinship behavior, joking
  relationships, 65, 79–80, 81–82;
  relationship to social classification,
  83–84

Laboratory of Anthropology of
  Santa Fe, 12
Lipan Apache, 8, 50, 93; absence
  of affinal avoidance, 70 *n;* baby
  carrier, 88–89, 93; dress, 87–88;
  field work, 70
Local group, 39, 40, 58; as farming
  unit, 43
Locality, importance of, 38 *n*

Mandelbaum, David, 79
Masked dancer ceremony, used to
  bring rain, 43
Masked dancers, 34; headdresses,
  19 *n*
Massey, Janice, 7
Mekeel, Scudder, 75 *n*
Mescal, 34. *See also* Agave
Mescalero Apache, 8, 25, 50;
  dress, 91
Mesquite beans, 58
Mexico, Apache in, 48, 50, 55, 62
Mogollón Mountain, 29
Mohave Apache, 32
Mule Mountains, 29

Navajo, 31, 71; agricultural
  practices, 54–55; clans, 39,
  40; degree of nomadism, 58;
  historical relation to Western
  Apache, 35 *n;* puberty rite, 23
Nicholas, Dan, 94
Northern Tonto Apache, 20 *n*,
  53, 67; differences in kinship
  usage, 79. *See also* Southern
  Tonto Apache; Tonto Apache

Parsons, Elsie Clews, 21 *n*
Payment for damages, 69
Peloncillo Mountains, 29
Peridot, Arizona, 76
Picurís, New Mexico, 92, 92 *n*
Pima Indians, 44
Piñon nuts, 58
Plants, considered hair of Earth, 34
Point of Pines, Arizona, 26
Population estimates, 53
Pottery, 63
Provinse, John, 34 *n*

Radcliffe-Brown, A. R., 13
Reagan, Albert B., 30 *n*
Reichard, Gladys A., 70
Rio Grande, 29

San Carlos, Arizona, 20
San Carlos Apache, 76. *See also* Arivaipa Apache
San Carlos River, 77
San Juan Mountain, Mexico, 29
San Pedro River, 28
Santa Rita Mountains, 29
Sapir, Edward, 30
Sayles, Theodore, 90
Shamanism, 52–53
Sinew-backed bow, 28
Snake, association of with agriculture, 45, 58
Social units, 37 *n*. *See also* Local group; Subtribal groups
Son-in-law obligation, 23
Sororate, 27
Southern Tonto Apache, 20 *n*, 76. *See also* Northern Tonto Apache; Tonto Apache
Southwest Society, 12
Spring haircutting ceremony, 27

Subtribal groups, 20 *n;* location of, 22
Sweat bath, 28
Sycamore tree, related to Sun, 34

Tax, Sol, 12
Tombstone, Arizona, 29
Tonkawa Indians, 95
Tonto Apache, 20, 71. *See also* Northern Tonto Apache; Southern Tonto Apache
Turkey, associated with corn, 51

Victory dance, 27

Warm Springs Apache, 24, 25. *See also* Chiricahua Apache
Western Apache, 50
Wheelwright, Mary C., 93
White Mountain Apache, 20 *n*, 71, 76; clans, 86; religion, 86. *See also* Coyotero Apache
White River, 63, 76

Yavapai Indians, 53
Yuma Apache, 32

Zuni Indians, 44, 45, 52